Abschlussprüfung Englisch

Realschule Baden-Württemberg

Cornelsen

LERNTIPPS

Liebe Schülerin, lieber Schüler!

Ab dem Schuljahr 2004/2005 wurde in Baden-Württemberg eine neue Prüfungsform für die schriftliche Abschlussprüfung im Fach Englisch an Realschulen eingeführt.

Die Musteraufgaben in diesem Übungsheft richten sich nach dieser neuen Form. Sie sollen dich – ebenso wie die folgenden Lerntipps – gezielt auf die Prüfung vorbereiten.

Die schriftliche Prüfung umfasst fünf Aufgabenbereiche:

A. **Text-based tasks** (Aufgaben zur Überprüfung des Textverständnisses)
B. **Use of language** (Aufgaben zu Wortschatz und Grammatik)
C. **Creative Writing** (Verfassen eigener Textbeiträge)
D. **Skills and Techniques** (Informationsentnahme und -weitergabe, Übersetzen)
E. **Spelling check** (Aufgaben zur zusätzlichen Überprüfung der Rechtschreibleistung)

Die Arbeitszeit für die schriftliche Prüfung beträgt 150 Minuten. Du kannst 100 Punkte erreichen. Dafür (auch noch für 95,5 Punkte!) bekommst du die Note 1,0. Bei 78 Punkten wird die Note 2,0 erteilt, und bei 60 Punkten die Note 3,0. Bei 50 Punkten weist der Bewertungsschlüssel die Note 3,5 aus, und bei 40 Punkten gibt es noch die Note 4,0. (Weniger als 40 Punkte wirst du vermutlich nicht erhalten, wenn du die Musteraufgaben des Heftes gründlich erarbeitest, und wenn du diese Lerntipps beachtest!)

Die Punkte verteilen sich nicht gleichmäßig auf die fünf Aufgabenbereiche der Prüfung. Für den E-Teil erhältst du beispielsweise weniger Punkte als für die anderen vier Teile. Dabei solltest du aber beachten, dass deine Rechtschreibleistung nicht nur dort, sondern auch in den englischsprachigen Aufgabenteilen A – D gewertet wird. Für sinnentstellende Fehler (z. B. bei Verwechslung von *then* und *than*) wird ein ganzer Punkt abgezogen. Bei nicht sinnentstellenden Fehlern erfolgt der Abzug eines halben Punktes (z. B. *easyly* anstatt *easily*).

Der C-Teil *(Creative Writing)* ist besonders wichtig. Hier kannst du die meisten Punkte erreichen. Aufgepasst beim *'story writing'* oder beim *'letter writing'!* Dort bemisst sich die Bewertung der sprachlichen Leistung nach inhaltlichen und sprachlichen Kriterien, die bei einer sehr guten Leistung so aussehen:

- *Inhalt entspricht den Anforderungen in besonderem Maße und ist situativ sehr gut gelungen*
- *erweiterter Wortschatz, idiomatische Ausdrucksweise*
- *grammatikalisch korrekt und abwechslungsreich im Satzbau*

Bitte unbedingt beachten: Bei inhaltlich oder situativ falscher Aussage gibt es für die gesamte Aufgabe 0 Punkte (selbst wenn sprachlich alles in Ordnung sein sollte!).

Sollte dir bei diesem Teil des *'Creative Writing'* die Aufgabenform nicht zusagen, so gibt es eine Alternative, auf die deutlich hingewiesen wird: "*Choose task 2a)* ***or*** *2b). Do* ***not*** *work on both tasks.*"

Wichtig ist, dass du die zur Verfügung stehende Arbeitszeit von 150 Minuten gut einteilst. Eine grobe Richtschnur kann dir dabei die Punkteverteilung für die einzelnen Aufgaben bieten. Wenn es zum Beispiel für die beiden Aufgabenteile A und B zusammen 45 Punkte gibt, müsstest du – da in diesem Falle noch 55 Punkte für die Teile C, D und E zu erreichen sind – nach der Hälfte der Arbeitszeit (also nach 75 Min.) bereits mit der Arbeit am C-Teil begonnen haben!

Abschlussprüfung Englisch

Lösungsheft

Realschule
Baden-Württemberg

Cornelsen

Lösungen zu den Aufgaben innerhalb der Lerntipps

Seite 4

'working as an au pair' (Lösungsvorschlag – andere Lösungen sind möglich):

1. Do you think I'm old enough to work as an au pair?
2. Are there enough jobs?
3. Where did you work?
4. How big was your family?
5. Did you have enough free time?

Seite 4

'Please fill in the correct forms of the verb ...'

1. goes
2. met
3. hadn't seen
4. asked
5. has phoned
6. hasn't given
7. is waiting
8. will be

Seite 5

'Read the text and write down the words ...'

1. ask
2. going
3. extremely
4. don't like
5. had to
6. watching
7. as hard
8. do
9. easily
10. properly

suffixes

1. scientist
2. violence/violent
3. argument
4. difference/different
5. surprised
6. activity
7. foreigner
8. happiness

Seite 7

common mistakes

1. There are ...
2. ... for many years
3. ... taller than ...
4. ... needn't hurry ...
5. ... often go ...
6. Most kids ...
7. ... worked hard ...

8. Do you sometimes do ...
9. ... plays ... well
10. ... is ringing
11. This information is ...
12. ... a nurse
13. ... often plays ...
14. ... by a dog, ...
15. ... played ...
16. She enjoys speaking ...
17. We've been here ...
18. ... people who ...

Seite 8

translation exercise

1. Ihr Bruder kam gestern kurz vor Mitternacht nach Hause.
2. Sie fahren gerne Ski.
3. Ich schaute mir das Spiel im Fernsehen an.
4. Sie brauchte fünf Minuten, um dort hin zu kommen.
5. Wir machen das später.

Seite 9

spelling exercises

1 spot the spelling mistakes

1. began
2. ad
3. specialists
4. applied
5. October
6. butterflies
7. telephone call
8. taking

Seite 10

2 plural forms

1. tomatoes
2. children
3. parties
4. lives
5. women
6. sandwiches

3 3rd person singular

1. finishes
2. hurries
3. does
4. kisses
5. tidies
6. says
7. loses
8. watches

4 -ing forms
The correct spelling is: planning – preferring – coming – offering – controlling – swimming

5 -ing forms
fitting – travelling – lying – promising – hurrying – rising

6 simple past
robbed – planned – tidied – controlled – hurried – preferred

Seite 11

7 homophones
1. bored – board
2. where – wear
3. right – write
4. there – their
5. I – eye
6. threw – through
7. whether – weather
8. piece – peace

A. Text Based Tasks *page 17*

1
1. false
2. true
3. true
4. false

2
1. (It's) easy to make, easy to serve (and) more varied than the hamburger.
2. The Greeks ate 'plakuntos' (and) the Romans ate 'picea'.
3. (It was) the pizza capital of the world.

3 SUGGESTED QUESTIONS
1. What was the food like? / Was the food good?
2. Were you sometimes still hungry after a meal?
3. What did you have for breakfast?
4. Could you eat as much as you wanted?

B. Use of Language *page 18*

1
1. delivery
2. tiring
3. careful
4. slippery
5. dangerous
6. friendly
7. annoying
8. angrily
9. best
10. learning
11. have discovered
12. starving

2 SUGGESTED ANSWERS
1. This means that the pizza has existed for a long time.
2. This is the name given to the ingredients you put on a pizza base (ham, cheese, tomato, etc).
3. This means that the pizza was named after Queen 'Marguerita' as a mark of respect for her.
4. 'Century' means a period of 100 years.

3
1. gradually (line 7)
2. various (line 11)
3. similar (line 15)

C. Creative Writing *page 19*

1
1. Before I reach the backpack, I would first ask the other passengers if it belongs to anyone or if they had seen the person sitting there. Then I would go to the front of the bus and tell the driver. He would probably call the appropriate office at the bus station to take a closer look at the backpack. (59 words)

3. I would tell my mother that it wasn't my fault and that it was not fair to stop me from seeing my friends. I would promise not to come home late again and try and persuade her to change her mind. If she still didn't agree I would feel very cross and go up to my room. (57 words)

2 A. The origin of umbrella hats
A friend of my father's invented umbrella hats. He got the idea when he went out running near his house one day. He was wearing a cap because it was hot and sunny. But the sky became grey and it started to rain. He turned round and started to run home quickly but it rained harder and harder and he got very wet. So when he got home, he took his little daughter's toy umbrella and fixed it to a metal headband. He put it on his head and opened the umbrella. It was perfect! When his friends saw it, they wanted one, too, so he made one for all of them. And now the umbrella hat is famous everywhere. (125 words)

B. There's a new fast food restaurant near my school. You can get burgers and chips and also hotdogs and pizzas. They sell soft drinks, too. It's not very expensive and it's as good as the other fast food places in town. I don't like the tables and chairs much because they are bright red and yellow but the people who work there are very friendly. They know us quite well now because we often go there instead of staying at the canteen at school, especially when a class is cancelled after lunch. It gives us a long lunch-hour. There's a jukebox there and we listen to music but the best thing is the TV on the wall which has all the sports channels. (123 words)

D. Skills and Techniques *pages 20-21*

1 1. Beim 'Hamburger' handelt es sich um gekochtes Hackfleisch – ein Lieblingsgericht der Bürger von Hamburg, das zwischen zwei Brothälften serviert wird, damit man es leichter zu sich nehmen kann. 'Hot Dog' ist eine lange heiße Wurst , die urspünglich 'Dachshund' hieß. Die Wurst wird in einem Brötchen serviert.
2. Beide Gerichte kamen durch Einwanderer aus Deutschland in die USA.
3. Das kommt daher, dass der Earl of Sandwich, der dem Gericht seinen Namen gab, während des Glücksspiels keine Zeit für ausführliche Mahlzeiten hatte.
4. Wiederum waren es Immigranten, die diese Gerichte in die Staaten brachten, diesmal aus Italien. 'Pizza' bedeutet ursprünglich 'kleiner Kuchen' und 'Spaghetti' bedeutet 'kleine Schnüre'.

2 Die Pizza ist mit den Italienern zum Ende des 19. Jahrhunderts in die USA eingewandert. Die erste Pizzeria in den Vereinigten Staaten wurde 1905 von Gennaro Lombardi in der Spring Street $53^{1}/_{2}$ in New York eröffnet. Doch die Beliebtheit der Pizza steigerte sich rasant, als die amerikanischen Soldaten nach dem 2. Weltkrieg aus Italien heimkehrten und von diesem "phantastischen italienischen Gericht" schwärmten. Heutzutage sind die Amerikaner die größten Hersteller und Verbraucher der Pizza weltweit.

E. Spelling Check *page 21*

1 1. chief
2. niece
3. received
4. piece
5. ceiling
6. thief

A. Text Based Tasks *page 23*

1 SUGGESTED ANSWERS

1. she was eight years old.
2. they wouldn't be able to cheer up sick children / children wouldn't laugh / they'd be useless.
3. distracts them so that the nurses can do their job.

2

1. false
2. false
3. false
4. true
5. true
6. false

3 INDIVIDUAL ANSWERS

1. She is hard-working, caring and probably a very strong person.
2. They feel happy and, therefore, they feel much better.
3. They participate in events to raise money for the Theodora Children's Trust.

4 SUGGESTED QUESTIONS

1. Do you enjoy your work?
2. Are you sad when you see the sick children?
3. How many children do you see at the hospital?
4. How often do you go to the hospital?
5. Is it difficult to learn to be a clown doctor?

B. Use of Language *page 24*

1 This means...

1. ... to make your face look funny so that people laugh at you.
2. ... to grab another person's hand when you say 'hello' or 'good-bye'.
3. ... to make sad children feel happier.
4. ... to become good friends with someone.

2

1. left
2. had taught (had been teaching)
3. fascinated
4. description
5. poverty
6. interested
7. easily
8. wrote
9. replacement
10. beginning
11. heat
12. feeling
13. exciting

C. Creative Writing *page 25*

1 The Theodora Children's Trust is looking for an experienced clown to be a clown doctor.
A clown doctor:
- visits sick children in hospital and entertains them.
- must be funny and inventive and make children laugh.
- should understand sick children's problems and how they feel.
- must work with the nurses and doctors.

Please write to............ (54 words)

2 A. Dear Anna
I am exhausted today. Some new children have arrived at the hospital this week and some of them don't speak English. One little girl is from Bosnia. She is about eight years old and is very sweet. It's sad because she is very ill and cannot get medical treatment in her own country. Her mother and father don't have enough money to come to England with her so she is homesick. She likes me a lot and I try to cheer her up as much as I can. Sometimes she is too tired to smile. She has taught me some words in her own language like 'Hello' and 'Thank you'.
Write to me soon. Love Lucy (120 words)

B. The Theodora Children's Trust sends clowns into hospital to cheer up sick children. They are called clown doctors but they are not medical doctors. They visit the children and make them laugh. Many of the children are very ill. They often spend a long time in hospital and this makes them sad and depressed. When the clown doctors come and see them the children laugh at their funny games and tricks and this makes them feel better. The doctors and nurses often ask the clown doctors to be with the children when they have to have an injection or take horrible medicine. Clown doctors do an important job and The Theodora Trust needs money to send more of them into hospitals. (121 words)

D. Skills and Techniques *pages 26-27*

1 **Q** What exactly does the Theodora Children's Trust do?
A Der Theodora Children's Trust ist eine Organisation, die Clown doctors ausbildet und sie dann zu den einzelnen Krankenhäusern schickt, um dort die Kinder aufzumuntern.
Q How long has it existed now?
A Schon über zehn Jahre. Die ersten Clowns gingen bereits 1994 in ein großes Londoner Kinderkrankenhaus
Q What do Clown doctors learn during their training?
A Die Clown doctors bekommen eine medizinische Ausbildung, in der sie etwas über die Verfahren in Krankenhäuser, Infektionen und den Umgang mit kranken Kindern lernen. In ihrer künstlerischen Ausbildung lernen sie zudem Pantomime, Jonglieren, Luftballonfiguren basteln und viele andere Mittel, um Kinder zu unterhalten.
Q How many hospitals in Great Britain work with Clown doctors?
A Gegenwärtig arbeiten Clown doctors an etwa 10 britischen Krankenhäusern.

2 Clown in einem Krankenhaus zu sein ist sehr ermüdend, körperlich wie auch emotional. Wir müssen lernen, unsere Gefühle nicht zu zeigen, andernfalls wären wir nutzlos. Clown doctors sind empfindsam, aber diese Seite von ihnen wird von den meisten Menschen nicht wahrgenommen. Den Kindern gegenüber sind wir immerzu fröhlich. Ich lerne immer noch, mir selbst zuzugestehen, dass ich ab und zu traurig bin. Es gibt einzelne Kinder, die einem sehr vertraut werden. Derzeit arbeite ich mit einem sehr kranken Mädchen aus Bosnien, das kein Englisch spricht, weshalb das Lachen unsere gemeinsame Sprache ist. Sie musste unzählige Male zu Operationen wieder ins Krankenhaus und ich denke ständig an sie.

E. Spelling Check *page 27*

1
1. quarrelling
2. hurrying
3 boiling
4. winning
5. happening
6. changing

2
1. hear
2. break
3 waste
4. tails
5. stairs
6. weight

3

A. Text Based Tasks *page 29*

1
1. true
2. true
3 true
4. false

2
1. three hundred and ninety
2. The International Shark Attack File
3 (You should) stay calm (and) leave the water quickly and quietly.

3 EXAMPLE QUESTIONS

Did you see the shark before it attacked you?
What did the shark do to you?
How did you get out of the water?
Do you still go surfing?
Are you frightened?
What is the film about the incident called?

B. Use of Language *page 30*

1
1. difference
2. scientists
3. automatically
4. specially
5. marked
6. hungry
7. keeper(s)
8. thirsty
9. worried
10. herself
11. had saved
12. boiling

2
1. This is the name of the rubber covers on car wheels.
2. This means she had several operations in hospital.
3. The techniques fishermen use to catch fish.
4. A box or a bag of basic medical necessities like a bandage, plasters, antiseptic cream, etc.

3
1. below (line 12)
2. hard (line 19)
3. cruel (line 36)
4. growing (line 39)

C. Creative Writing *page 31*

1
1. If the person was in the water quite near the beach, I would try and pull him or her out. But if the person was a long way from the beach I would run as fast as I could to the nearest person on the beach and ask for help. I would ask them to phone the lifeguards or the police. (61 words)
3. I would go to see my friend who lives next door. I would explain the problem and ask if I could stay in his house until one of my family members came back. I would watch TV or play on the computer. If my friend was not at home, I would sit on the ground by the door and wait! (60 words)

2

A. Dear Jan
I'm having a great time here in Hawaii at a sports club. We go surfing every day and I am getting good at it! Some of the surfers are fantastic and they do incredible things riding the waves. We must be careful because there are sharks in the ocean! Yesterday there was a terrible accident. A champion surfer was attacked by a shark and lost her arm. She shouted loudly and her friends rushed into the water. Luckily they were able to save her and took her to hospital. She is lucky to be alive. I feel nervous now about going into the water so I sit on the beach and watch the other surfers.
See you soon. (120 words)

B. I was walking to my friend's house the other day when I saw a wallet on the pavement. I picked it up and opened it. There were some credit cards with the name 'Winston', a five pound note and a photo of a little boy in front of a house. Fortunately, I recognized the house, so I didn't have to search for the address. I went there and rang the bell. A lady opened the door. 'Are you Mrs Winston?', I asked her. 'Yes, I am,' she replied. I showed her the wallet. She was very surprised and looked inside it. Then she thanked me and put a note in my hand as a reward. I looked down. Ten pounds! More than a month's pocket money! (126 words)

D. Skills and Techniques *pages 32-33*

1
1. Man geht allgemein davon aus, dass das Surfen auf der Pazifikinsel Hawaii seinen Ursprung nahm. Schon vor langer Zeit war das Wellenreiten für die dortigen Fischer eine Art Zeitvertreib und sie bedienten sich zunächst einfacher Surfbretter aus Holz. Je besser einer surfen konnte, umso wichtiger und mächtiger wurde er und nur echte Könner wurden an die besten Küstenabschnitte gelassen.
2. Als Kaptain Cook die Insel 1778 entdeckte, wurde er auf diese Wellenreiter aufmerksam und war von ihrem Können beeindruckt. Dies ist in seinen Aufzeichnungen festgehalten.
3. Luau bezeichnet eine Tradition aus Hawaii: Es ist ein Fest, bei dem Schweine geröstet und süße Kartoffeln verzehrt werden. Als Drink dazu gibt es das so genannte Mai Tai. Alle Gäste werden dazu mit Girlanden geschmückt und the Frauen führen einen traditionellen Tanz auf.

2 Wenn die Surfer auf das Meer hinausschwimmen und nach einer großen Welle Ausschau halten, dann bewegen sie dabei das Brett mit Armen und Beinen über das Wasser. Von unten gesehen, also von dort wo die Haie sind, sehen die Surfer und ihre Bretter dann ähnlich aus wie Robben oder Schildkröten. Haie können nicht besonders gut sehen, daher greifen sie Surfer vermutlich nur aus Versehen an. Tatsächlich versuchen die Haie so gut wie nie, einen Surfer zu verspeisen, sobald sie merken, dass er oder sie nicht ihrer Lieblingsnahrung entspricht.

E. Spelling Check *page 33*

1
1. lorries
2. leaves
3. roofs
4. calves
5. peaches
6. mosquitoes

4

A. Text Based Tasks *page 35*

1
1. C
2. A
3 D
4. B
5. E

2
1. To celebrate the Earth and protest against pollution.
2. Rubbish, chemicals, smog and car exhaust.
3. They help people plan demonstrations, campaigns, talks, and other activities.
4. By organising clean-up campaigns, picking up rubbish or writing letters to rheir Council.

3 EXAMPLE QUESTIONS
Why are you marching?
Are there a lot of people?
Are you carrying a banner?
What is written on it?
Where are you marching to?
Do you think this will help the environment?

B. Use of Language *page 36*

1
1. wildest
2. particularly
3. peaceful
4. relaxing
5. impressive
6. exciting
7. rocky
8. useful
9. lost
10. traditional
11. comfortable
12. setting off

2
1. This is when people come together for a special occasion like a birthday or anniversary.
2. This means everything that people throw away.
3. This means the world around us.

3
1. purpose (line 3)
2. throughout (line 29)
3. participate (line 43)

C. Creative Writing *page 37*

1
2. I would follow the girl out of the shop and talk to her. I would tell her she shouldn't have done that and try and persuade her not to do it again. I would explain that stealing even small things was not fair on the shopkeeper. I would ask her how she would feel if someone stole something from her. (60 words)
3. First of all I would go down to the beach and look at the oil. Then I would ask if I could help to clean up the beach. I would ask some friends to come with me. I would put on my boots and my rain coat and spend the day on the beach rescuing birds and scraping oil off the rocks. (62 words)

2 A. Last week I went round the whole school from the top to the ground floor. In all the corridors, the lower part of the walls are cracked and dirty where pupils have kicked them. A lot of the desk tops in the classrooms have been damaged by sharp objects. In the toilets, there's graffiti on the doors and walls. In the playground, although there are plenty of rubbish bins, there are empty packets of biscuits and paper bags on the ground. I saw old scarves and gloves in the branches of the trees and the basket ball posts have been bent and damaged. And I found a maths and a geography book lying in the rain! Who do they belong to? (121 words)

B. The noise got louder and louder. I was intrigued so I got up and went over to the window. I parted the curtains and looked out. I saw the strangest vehicle. It was a big old-fashioned lorry with glass sides. And through the glass I could see two lions walking up and down in the small space, looking out into the road. On the top of the lorry was a big notice saying 'Barnum's Circus is coming to your town. Don't miss it!'. The loudspeaker was playing loud music and the man next to the driver was speaking into a microphone at the same time. It was a terrible noise and nobody could hear a word he was saying! (120 words)

D. Skills and Techniques *page 38*

1
1. Man kann schon Einfluss nehmen, indem man über die Umweltproblematik spricht und darüber hinaus versucht, sich selbst möglichst umweltfreundlich zu verhalten.
2. Anstatt sich mit dem Auto fahren zu lassen, kann man genau so gut zu Fuß gehen oder mit dem Fahrrad fahren. Man kann car-sharing organisieren, das heißt sein eigenes Auto in Nutzergemeinschaften mit anderen teilen. Schließlich kann man seine Eltern durchaus dazu anhalten, sämtliche Besorgungen auf einmal zu erledigen, sodass mehrere Autofahrten entfallen.
3. Die Herstellung von Plastiktüten ist sehr umweltbelastend und es dauert viele Jahre, bis sie natürlich abgebaut werden.
4. Es ist ganz einfach: Es genügt die Produktbeschreibungen genau zu lesen und möglichst Produkte mit hohen chemischen Anteilen zu meiden.
5. Weil wir schlicht Teil dieser Natur sind. Das Gleichgewicht der Natur zu stören heißt unsere eigene Umwelt zu gefährden.

2 Stell dir einen Tag vor, an dem 500 Millionen Menschen aus 184 Ländern der ganzen Welt zusammenkommen, um für einen einzigen Zweck zu feiern und zu protestieren. Genau das ist am 22. April 2000 geschehen. An diesem Tag war 'Earth Day' und der Zweck, den diese Leute im Sinn hatten, war, etwas für eine gesündere und sicherere Welt für jeden Einzelnen zu tun. Es war die größte Veranstaltung dieser Art in der Geschichte der Menschheit.

E. Spelling Check *page 39*

1
1. tyre
2. diary
3. forbidden
4. break
5. storey
6. lose

5

A. Text Based Tasks page 41

1
1. (He is) a sailing instructor.
2. Seb liked to spend his free time with his dad.
3. Seb spent every free moment training for the race.
4. The boats were identical.
5. They sailed from Tenerife, Spain to Antigua.
6. Seb's dad won the race.

2
1. Ben
2. Seb
3. Giorgina
4. Catherine
5. Ben
6. Giorgina

3 EXAMPLE QUESTIONS

How long did it take you?
What was the weather like?
Did you have any storms?
How did you manage to sleep?
What did you eat?
Were you afraid?
Were you lonely?
Could you see your father's boat?
Would you like to do it again?

B. Use of Language pages 42-43

1
1. confident
2. experienced
3. challenging
4. courageous
5. competitive
6. convenient

2
1. set sail (line 12)
2. aboard (line 15)
3. a solo voyage (line 20)
4. to express your thoughts (line 36)
5. the chance (line 41)
6. no wonder (line 54-55)

3 1. by – in
2. in – to
3. until – to
4. all days – every day
5. at – to
6. Each – All
7. hold – held
8. in – at

C. Creative Writing *page 43*

1 1. I agree that sailing is a sport for rich people. It isn't a simple sport where you just need your hands and feet and a ball. You need a boat. And boats are very expensive to buy. And when you are not sailing in it, it costs a lot to rent a space to keep it in the harbour. (59 words)
2. I think sailing is one of the most exciting and interesting sports. It's a sport where there is a lot of variety and you have to be good at doing many things. You need to be physically fit because there is a lot of climbing and pulling to do. Also, you have to know how to use all the technical equipment on board. (63 words)

2 A. Hi Fran
I've just come back from holiday club. I had a really good time. I was in a room with three others and we had a lot of fun. During the day there were lots of things to do. We went sailing and I learnt to water-ski! It's not easy! We also went hang-gliding – it's fantastic but I was a bit nervous at first! The food was quite good. We had a picnic at midday and a barbecue in the evening. We had to help with the washing-up afterwards! I played ping pong a lot and in the evening we played board games. We had a great party on the last evening!
Hope you had a good holiday, too. (120 words)

B. Last year on holiday, some friends invited us to go sailing with them on their yacht but my sister wasn't well so we couldn't go. Our friends went off by themselves for the day. It was very hot and in the afternoon the sky became very dark and there was a terrible storm. The thunder roared and the lightning flashed. We thought about our friends at sea and hoped they had come back. The next day we didn't see them and we couldn't see their boat in the port. We were worried. We saw them three days later and learnt that they had been rescued by the lifeboat and had spent two days in hospital. Thank goodness we hadn't gone with them! (122 words)

D. Skills and Techniques *pages 44-45*

1 1. Ellen ist in Zentralengland aufgewachsen, weit ab von der Küste. Als sie acht Jahre alt war, nahm ihre Tante sie auf einen Segeltörn mit. Von diesem Moment an war sie für den Sport begeistert.
2. Drei Jahre lang hatte sie auf ihr erstes Boot gespart und ihre Großmutter legte noch etwas dazu.
3. Mit 18 Jahren gewann Ellen den Young Sailor of the Year Award. Danach beteiligte sie sich an mehreren internationalen Rennen und gewann den Titel Yachtsman of the Year. Schließlich gewann sie, 25-jährig, das Vendée-Globe-Rennen.
4. Während des Vendée-Globe-Rennens war Ellen vollkommen auf sich selbst gestellt. Sie musste selbstständig Reparaturen durchführen, Seestürme bewältigen und Eisberge umschiffen. Zudem musste sie gegen ihre Erschöpfung ankämpfen und dabei ständig Kurs halten.
5. Ellen nimmt Kinder, die an Krebserkrankungen leiden, zu Segeltouren mit. Ein Foto von einem dieser Kinder – es ist das Bild eines lächelnden Mädchens – begleitet sie auf ihren Reisen.

2 Eines Tages sagte Sebs Mutter zu ihm und zu seinem Vater: "Ihr seid beide so ehrgeizig. Warum macht ihr nicht ein Rennen, um herauszufinden, wer der bessere Segler ist?" Sie machte nur Spaß, aber Seb und Ian nahmen die Idee durchaus ernst. Während der folgenden drei Jahre trainierte Seb jede freie Minute mit seinem Vater, und am 19. Dezember 2002 setzte Seb in Teneriffa, Spanien, die Segel zum größten Abenteuer seines Lebens: einem Rennen gegen seinen Vater über den Atlantik.

E. Spelling Check *page 45*

1
1. cycling
2. canoeing
3. running
4. skating
5. skiing
6. swimming

2
1. explanation
2. expression
3. politician
4. direction
5. explosion
6. electrician

6

A. Text Based Tasks *page 47*

1
1. he didn't fit in with other kids.
2. he went to university.
3. young, multiracial people.
4. other people of mixed race and their experiences.
5. gives support to multiracial teens and their families.

2
1. Because he has a Korean mother and a white father.
2. white, black, Asian and Hispanic kids.
3. They are encouraged to write their own stories about being multiracial.

3
1. How many pupils of mixed racial backgrounds are there at your school?
2. What kind of activities do they like doing in their leisure time?
3. Do they fit in with the other pupils who are not multiracial?
4. What are their main problems which are related to being multiracial?
5. What is their attitude concerning professional life after leaving school?

B. Use of Language *page 48*

1
1. I'm sorry but I disagree with your idea.
2. Keep still! Don't be impatient!
3. Our new neighbour is very unfriendly.
4. In Sweden it's illegal for parents to slap their children.
5. I dislike cleaning and tidying my room.
6. In Japan it's impolite to wear your shoes in the house.

2
1. integrate (line 14)
2. he asked himself (line 17)
3. problems they shared (line 21)
4. origins (line 35)

3
1. teenagers (line 4)
2. confused (line 16)
3. he realized (line 22)
4. he founded (line 25)
5. dated (line 34)
6. celebrities (line 36)

C. Creative Writing *page 49*

1
1. I would explain to the ticket seller that I had forgotten my card and I would ask him or her to let me have the reduction. I would tell him how old I was and which school I went to. If the person refused I wouldn't buy a normal ticket. I would come back to see the film it another time. (62 words)
2. I would go up to her during the break and ask her if she wanted some help. I would try to explain in simple words and sign language. I would try to be friends with her and ask the teacher if I could sit next to or near her in class so that I could explain things she didn't understand. (60 words)

2

A. We have a new boy in class called James. He's from Edinburgh in Scotland and he speaks with a strong Scottish accent. Last week, James brought his father's kilt to school for World Day. This is a short tartan skirt that Scottish men often wear on special occasions. James asked me if I wanted to try it on so I took off my jeans and put on the kilt. Then I stood on the desk and tried to do a Scottish dance. Everyone laughed. Just then, the head teacher walked in. I was so embarrassed. She looked at me and then said,' Are you going to play us the bagpipes?'. If not, you'd better take off your kilt and sit down! (121 words)

B. Dear Gary
We had World Day at school last week. This is a day when each class organizes an activity based on different traditions in countries all over the world. Our class cooked food from Asian countries. We made some Japanese sushi – that's raw fish and rice, Chinese chop suey and spicy chicken from Thailand. Another class played South American Indian music with reed pipes and small drums. They wore brightly coloured clothes from Peru and Mexico. Form 5 dressed up in clothes from India and Africa. The girls wore Indian saris and the boys wore long cotton tunics. Other classes presented food from the Middle East and music from the West Indies like Jamaica.
Does your school have World Day? Write and tell me, please. (123 words)

D. Skills and Techniques *pages 50-51*

1 1. 'MAVIN' ist der Name der 4-mal jährlich erscheinenden Zeitschrift. Die MAVIN Foundation hingegen fördert und organisiert Projekte für Menschen unterschiedlicher Hautfarbe.
2. Bei der Generation MIX tour ging es um eine Busreise, die 5 Teenager aus dem multikulturellen Bereich durch die USA unternahmen. Sie wollten dabei mit möglichst vielen Menschen über Fragen, die mit ihrer Hautfarbe zu tun haben, ins Gespräch kommen.
3. Das Matchmaker Bone Marrow Projekt hilft, Organübertragungen für Menschen unterschiedlicher Herkunft und Rasse möglich zu machen.
4. Bei Menschen, die aus unterschiedlichen Rassen abstammen, ist die genetische Zusammensetzung oft sehr speziell, weshalb es schwieriger ist, geeignete Spenderorgane zu finden.
5. Es handelt sich dabei um ein Buch, das Familien mit Kindern unterschiedlicher Abstammung viele Ratschläge und Informationen zu Themen wie Gesundheit oder Erziehung gibt.

2 Als Matt Kaley in den Vereinigten Staaten aufwuchs, stellte er sich oft die Frage "Wer bin ich eigentlich?" Daran ist natürlich nichts Ungewöhnliches; die meisten Teenager stellen von Zeit zu Zeit genau diese Frage. Doch Matts Problem war ein ganz besonderes. Wenn er seine Mitschüler betrachtete, konnte er keinen finden, der so aussah wie er. Es gab weiße und schwarze, asiatische und hispanic kids, aber keines sah so aus wie er. Wenn er dann nach Hause ging und den Fernseher anschaltete oder eine Zeitschrift aufschlug, sah er noch immer niemanden, der so war wie er selbst.

E. Spelling Check *page 51*

1 1. whose – week
2. weather – we're
3. past – their
4. write – here
5. piece – meat
6. allowed – hair

7

A. Text Based Tasks *page 53*

1 1. above up to
2. walk drive
3. all afternoon two hours
4. top foot
5. seven a couple of (OR two)
6. through the rain forest along the beach
7. along the beach through the rain forest
8. read about seen on television
9. down to the top of
10. the evening midday
11. shallow full (OR deep)
12. full shallow
13. only just managed to drive across drove across easily

2 1. Because they want to build holiday homes.
2. There should be strict laws that prevent them from doing this.
3. The forests will slowly be destroyed.
4. I think they are very, very stupid.

3 1. Where have you been and what have you done?
2. What's the rain forest like?
3. Are you and your father getting on well?
4. Are you enjoying being with him?

B. Use of Language *pages* 54-55

1 1. quickly
2. fantastic (OR wonderful)
3. love
4. angrily
5. improved
6. to cheer up

2 1. imagination
2. explorers
3. length
4. variety
5. memorable
6. friendly
7. playful
8. brightly
9. sandy
10. ensure
11. tourists

3 1. across
2. out of
3. through
4. along
5. over
6. onto

C. Creative Writing *pages* 55-56

1 You should take a backpack with a bottle of water and a pair of sunglasses. It's also useful to take some binoculars. You should wear shorts and a T-shirt, and walking shoes with cotton socks (take your shoes off and tie them round your neck when walking through water). Don't forget to wear a cap or a sunhat. (59 words)

2 A. Bob: I'm going to build a house.
Tom: But if you cut down trees, you will slowly destroy the forest.
Bob: But the rain forest is enormous. A few trees won't change anything!
Tom: But thousands of people have already cut down millions of trees!
Bob: Why does that matter?
Tom: Because the rain forest is important to us. It produces a lot of the oxygen that we breathe and contains fresh water.
Bob: There's oxygen and fresh water all over the world!
Tom: But there will be much less if rain forests are destroyed And there are millions of birds and animals which live in the rain forest.
Bob: I'm not going to kill any animals!
Tom: But if the rain forest disappears, so will they. They need the rain forest to survive.
(128 words)

B. Dear Dad
This is to thank you for a great holiday in Australia. I shall never forget the fantastic things we did. I loved the trip to the rain forest and learning all about it. It was fun to see the crocodiles in the reserve, too. The most exciting part of the holiday was sailing out to the Great Barrier Reef. Do you remember those amazing dolphins swimming along with the boat? I took some really good photos of them. I'll send them to you. I have put my shells and pieces of coral on the shelf in my room. Thanks again for giving me such a good time. Good Luck with the 'Save the Rain Forest' campaign! Write to me soon. (118 words)

D. Skills and Techniques *pages 56-57*

1 1. Hast du gewusst, dass der amazonische Regenwald 20 % des weltweiten Sauerstoffs produziert und etwa 30 % der weltweiten Trinkwasserreserven birgt? Außerdem findet man dort eine einmalige Artenvielfalt und zahlreiche medizinisch wertvolle Pflanzen. Stell dir vor: 60 % aller Medikamente gegen Krebs und andere lebensgefährliche Krankheiten werden aus Pflanzen gewonnen, die nur im Regenwald zu finden sind.
Nach und nach wird dieser Regenwald aber zerstört. Zum einen tun dies die Farmer, die immer mehr Land für ihre Rinderzucht benötigen, zum anderen aber sind es große Konzerne, die entweder das Holz verwerten oder in den Regenwäldern nach Öl bohren.
Dabei sind die Regenwälder nicht einmal in privatem Besitz. Sie sind öffentliches Land und in vielen Teilen leben sogar noch Menschen.
Die Leute, die dieses Flugblatt hier geschrieben haben, verlangen deshalb, dass dieser Raubbau aufhört. Das kann nur geschehen, wenn es entsprechende Gesetze gibt, die den Regenwald und die dort lebenden Menschen nachhaltig schützen.

Translation
Als sie den Regenwald hinter sich gelassen hatten und die Straßen besser wurden, besserte sich Toms Stimmung. Er erzählte Alex alles über die 'Gipsy Woman', das Boot, das er mit seinem Bruder teilte und das in Cairns vor Anker lag.
"Ich dachte, wir könnten sie zum Riff rausbringen", sagte er.
"Zum Great Barrier Riff?" ,sagte Alex ganz aufgeregt.
"Genau das meine ich", lachte Tom.
Alex grinste. Natürlich wusste er alles über das Great Barrier Riff. Er hatte davon schon im Geographieunterricht gehört und wollte immer einmal das farbenprächtige Riff mit eigenen Augen sehen. Genau das würde er jetzt tun.
"Ist es denn so wunderbar, wie es im Film aussieht?" ,fragte er.
"Besser", antwortete Tom. "Millionenfach besser."

E. Spelling Check *page 57*

1
1. Here's
2. Jane's bike's Who's
3. it's
4. pupils'
5. men's women's children's
6. There's James' today's

8

A. Text Based Tasks *page 59*

1 SUGGESTED QUESTIONS
1. How long did it take you to build and plan the bridge?
2. When did the bridge open?
3. Who collaborated with you?
4. How high is the bridge?
5. How long is the bridge?
6. What are the important aspects of the design of the bridge?
7. How much impact did the construction have on the environment?
8. What is your philosophy concerning architecture?

2
1. The traffic had to go down one side of the valley, cross the old bridge over the Tarn river, and then go up the other side of the valley.
2. There were terrible traffic jams particularly in the summer.
3. Because this would not have solved the problem of traffic jams and environmental damage.
4. He decided to build a bridge which linked the two high plateaus on each side of the River Tarn.
5. It has shortened the journey by two hours.

3
1. engineers architects
2. link Paris to the Mediterranean
3. It is one of the longest road bridges of its type and the single tallest road bridge in the world.
4. the surrounding landscape
5. to the environment

B. Use of Language *pages 60-61*

1
1. In this context it means a very simple, basic design
2. to connect
3. huge, enormous
4. complete disorder and confusion

2
1. OK
2. most
3. in
4. being
5. OK
6. OK
7. to
8. one
9. do
10. to
11. OK
12. OK
13. of
14. there
15. OK
16. OK

3
1. widened
2. heightened
3. lengthened
4. enlarged
5. hardens
6. strengthen

C. Creative Writing *page 61*

1
1. You should make sure your front and back lights work. You should always wear a reflective band across your chest and back. It's even better to wear a reflective jacket. If you carry a backpack, choose one which has reflective bands on it. You should cycle near the side of the road so that cars can overtake you easily. (59 words)
2. It is not a good idea to take it to school. If you do, always carry it around with you in your pocket. Don't leave it in a bag or a locker. Remember to turn it off when you are in class. The teacher may confiscate it if it rings during a lesson! Buy a cover for it to protect it. (61 words)
3. The best thing to do is to look on the internet for a list of canoeing clubs. Then choose a club in an area you like – maybe on the coast, or perhaps on a river - and phone them. Ask them if they do canoeing courses during the summer holidays and how much they are. They will send you papers to fill in. (63 words)

2 A. article

In the old part of my town there are a lot of old buildings which are at least four hundred years old. One of them is called 'The Red House' because is it made of red brick. The building is not straight; it leans a little over the road. There are statues over each window and a big carved stone over the main door with writing on it. There are wooden beams in the walls and the door is made of carved wood. Inside, the floors are made of stone and they are not very even. The walls have been painted with patterns of leaves and symbols around the top and there is a big open fireplace in each room. (120 words)

Du findest im Anhang dieser Lerntipps eine Liste von Arbeitsanweisungen, die häufig in Prüfungsaufgaben vorkommen. Bei der Lösung der Musteraufgaben dieses Heftes solltest du in der Liste nachschauen, wenn du eine Anweisung nicht verstehst, oder wenn du ein wichtiges Wort vergessen hast.

Wenn du alle Musteraufgaben dieses Heftes bearbeitet hast, kannst du in Form der Selbsteinschätzung überprüfen, ob deine Fähigkeiten, Fertigkeiten und Kenntnisse wohl zu einer guten oder zufrieden stellenden Prüfungsleistung führen werden. (siehe: *Teste dich selbst* im Anhang)

Nun aber zu den einzelnen Aufgabenbereichen der Prüfung:

A. Text-based tasks

Grundlage für verschiedene Arbeitsaufgaben ist der Basistext, den du stets auf der ersten Seite des Aufgabensatzes findest, und der ungefähr 400 Wörter umfasst.

Beschäftige dich zunächst intensiv mit diesem Text. Gehe nicht zu schnell an die Arbeitsaufgaben auf den weiteren Seiten heran! Nicht nur im A-Teil, sondern auch in anderen Aufgabenteilen greift man nämlich immer wieder auf den Basistext zurück. Beispielsweise werden im B-Teil manchmal Aufgaben im Zusammenhang mit den im Text auf Seite 1 vorkommenden Wörtern gestellt. Außerdem wird in der Regel der Übersetzungstext des D-Teils dem Ausgangstext entnommen.

Lies also zunächst den Ausgangstext mindestens zweimal gut durch. Beim ersten Lesen wirst du herausfinden, wovon der Text handelt. Es ist ganz normal, wenn du nicht gleich alles verstehst. Beim zweiten oder dritten Lesen wirst du die Bedeutung vieler Wörter und Begriffe erschließen können, welche dir anfänglich unbekannt waren. Hilfreich ist es, wenn du dir überlegst, in welchem Zusammenhang die Wörter stehen, oder wenn du an die entsprechende Wortfamilie denkst. Häufig hilft die deutsche oder eine andere Sprache beim Verstehen des Begriffes.

Während des zweiten oder dritten Lesens könntest du dir wichtig erscheinende Textstellen farbig markieren. Vergiss nicht, dir Notizen zu machen, z. B. der folgenden Art:

- ***Who*** *did what?*
- ***Where*** *or* ***when*** *did she/he do it?*
- ***How*** *and* ***why*** *did it happen?*

Nach dem gründlichen Lesen und Erfassen des Textes kannst du an die Bearbeitung der Aufgaben gehen. Diese *text-based tasks* bestehen zunächst aus Fragen zum Ausgangstext. Die Antworten auf die Fragen können teilweise direkt dem Text entnommen werden. Die Reihenfolge der gestellten Fragen entspricht dabei der Reihenfolge der Textabschnitte. Bei den Antworten sind nur dann vollständige Sätze zu schreiben, wenn ausdrücklich darauf hingewiesen wird. *('Write your answers in complete sentences'.)*

Bei deinen Antworten auf die Fragen, die sich auf den Text beziehen, darfst du nicht zu viel dem Ausgangstext entnehmen. Du bekommst keinen Punkt, wenn du einen gesamten Textabschnitt abschreibst, nur weil du dort die richtige Antwort vermutest!

Manchmal beziehen sich nicht alle gestellten Fragen direkt auf den betreffenden Text. Dann wirst du darauf hingewiesen *('The answers needn't be in the text.')*.

Gelegentlich sollst du angefangene Sätze mit Hilfe des Ausgangstextes vervollständigen: *'Finish the sentences.'* Oder du musst entscheiden, ob vorgegebene Antworten, die sich auf den Text beziehen, richtig oder falsch sind: *'Decide whether the following statements are right or wrong.'*

Im A-Teil der schriftlichen Prüfung wird überprüft, ob du englische Fragen bilden kannst. Nachdem du das in den vorhergehenden Schuljahren oft geübt hast, kannst du dabei nicht mehr viel falsch machen.

Häufig werden bei Aufgabenstellungen zur Fragebildung nur wenige Vorgaben gemacht, das heißt, dass du dir nicht nur überlegen musst, ***wie*** du den Partner fragen kannst, sondern auch ***was*** du wissen möchtest:

You want to work as an au pair in Great Britain. Your pen friend from Manchester did so some time ago. Ask her or him about being an au pair. Use at least three different question forms. [1]

Beachte bitte den Hinweis im letzten Satz der obigen Arbeitsanweisung! Bildest du deine Fragen alle nach dem gleichen sprachlichen Muster, so verschenkst du Punkte.

Sobald du mit dem A-Teil fertig bist, solltest du alle Antworten durchlesen. Korrigiere die inhaltlichen und sprachlichen Fehler und achte besonders auf die Rechtschreibung. Bei falscher Schreibweise werden dir Punkte abgezogen! Wenn du dir nicht ganz sicher bist, ersetze das betreffende Wort durch ein anderes, das du besser kennst.

B. Use of language

Im zweiten Teil der schriftlichen Prüfung werden Aufgaben zu Wortschatz und Grammatik gestellt *('Vocabulary and grammar').*

Die Wortschatzaufgaben sind häufig Einsetzübungen. Du musst dabei Wörter so in die Satzlücken einfügen, dass der Satz einen Sinn ergibt und alles sprachlich korrekt ist:

'Write down the words in brackets in the correct form: 'It was ... cold outside. (terrible)'

Du hast sicher erkannt, dass hier das Adverb *'terribly'* eingefügt werden muss.

Bei den Aufgaben zur Überprüfung der Grammatik-Kenntnisse handelt es sich häufig um eine Übung zum richtigen Gebrauch der Zeitformen im Englischen *('use of tenses').* Die Schwierigkeit liegt u. a. in der unterschiedlichen Anwendung der einzelnen Zeitformen in den beiden Sprachen. Wo wir beispielsweise im Deutschen das Present Perfect verwenden *(„Gestern bin ich daheim gewesen."),* steht im Englischen das *Simple Past ("Yesterday I was at home.").*

Es lohnt sich, bei Aufgabenstellungen zum Gebrauch der Zeiten genau zu überlegen, in welchem zeitlichen Zusammenhang die entsprechende Aussage steht. Dazu empfiehlt sich die Suche nach typischen Signalwörtern, die meist einen eindeutigen Hinweis auf die richtige Zeitform geben. Im obigen Beispiel weist das Wort *'yesterday'* darauf hin, dass das 'simple past' verwendet wird.

Wenn du in den folgenden Sätzen jeweils auf das Signalwort achtest, wirst du die Lösung leichter finden. (Allerdings wird das Signalwort in den Prüfungsaufgaben leider nicht unterstrichen sein – du wirst es selbst finden müssen!)

Please fill in the correct forms of the verbs given in brackets: [2]

*My brother 1. ... (go) to the same disco **every week**. **Last week** he 2. .... (meet) a girl called Vicky. He 3. ... (not see) her at the disco **before**. **On Monday** my brother 4. ... (ask) Vicky to his 18th birthday party. It's next weekend. He 5. ... (phone) her twice this week **so far**, but she 6. ... (not give) him an answer **yet**. **Now** he 7. ... (wait) for her to call. **If** she doesn't phone him soon, he 8. ... (be) very sad.*

1 *Die Lösungen bzw. die Lösungsvorschläge für diese und die weiteren Übungsaufgaben findest du im beiliegenden Lösungsheft.*
2 *Shortened and adapted from : Practice Book zur 'Cornelsen English Grammar', Kompaktausgabe, Cornelsen 2004, S. 151*

Oft sind die Aufgaben zu Wortschatz und Grammatik zu einer einzigen Übung zusammengefasst. Dann ist es für das Textverständnis besonders wichtig, die Übung vor dem Ausfüllen der Lücken gut durchzulesen.

Read the text and write down the words in brackets in the correct form. [1]

... Sometimes people ... (1. ask) me, "Why should I learn a foreign language? I'm not interested in ... (2. go) abroad anyway. I can't get the food I like, everything is ... (3. extreme) expensive, and people abroad usually ... (4. not/like) tourists anyway." – "But even if you don't go abroad, languages are important. They've often been useful for me when I ... (5. must) talk to foreigners at work. And today, ... (6. watch) foreign TV programmes isn't ... (7. hard) with a satellite dish. Millions of people ... (8. do) it every year. Today videos and computer programmes help you to learn the pronunciation more ... (9. easy), which is important if you want to speak the language ... (10. proper)."

Bei den Übungen zum Wortschatz musst du häufig einen im Ausgangstext vorkommenden Begriff in einem Satz erklären. Beispiel: Du sollst in einem Text über den tropischen Regenwald den Begriff *'forest'* erklären. Das geht natürlich nur, wenn du weißt, dass *'forest'* im Deutschen ‚Wald' heißt. (Keine Sorge vor unbekannten Wörtern – oft darfst du aus vier oder fünf Begriffen zwei oder drei auswählen, die du dann sicher kennst!) Nun gibt es verschiedene Möglichkeiten, an die Aufgabe heran zu gehen.

a) Du gibst eine Definition des Wortes 'forest': *"A forest is a part of the landscape where you can find a lot of trees."*
b) Du versuchst, einen Satz zu bilden, aus dem klar ersichtlich wird, dass der ‚Wald' gemeint ist. *("The wood we need for making furniture is mainly cut in the forest.").*
c) Du erreichst die entsprechende Punktzahl auch, wenn du ein Wort mit gleicher oder ähnlicher Bedeutung (Synonym) als Erklärung heranziehen kannst *("Forest means woodland (or woods).").*

Der umgekehrte Fall kommt ebenfalls vor. Es wird dir ein Wort oder eine Definition vorgegeben und du musst im Ausgangstext das Synonym finden: *"Find the words in the text that have more or less the same meaning."*

Auf die Übung *'Find the suitable forms of the words'* bist du sicher gut vorbereitet, da in den Lehrbüchern derartige Aufgaben häufig zu finden sind. Da sie nicht nur im B-Teil der Prüfung stehen können, sondern auch wichtig sind im Hinblick auf die korrekte Schreibung der Wörter, solltest du die nächste Übung genau anschauen:

Word building: Suffixes [2]

Complete the following words:
1. sci- 2. viol- 3. argu- 4. differ- 5. surprise- 6. active- 7. foreign- 8. happi-
You may use the following suffixes: -ence -ness -ed -ment -ent -ist -er -ity

C. Creative Writing

Hier sollst du zeigen, wie gut du englische Texte schreiben kannst. Du sollst beispielsweise deine Meinung zu einem Thema schriftlich darlegen *('What's your opinion?')*. Damit dir das gelingt, benötigst du einige wichtige Redewendungen:

Bei Zustimmung: *I agree (with the statement). – That's true. – That's right.*
Bei Ablehnung: *I can't agree (with ...). – That's not right. – I don't think you can say ... .*
Um die Meinung auszudrücken: *In my opinion ... . – I think ... .*
Für Begründungen: *First of all ..., second ..., and then/finally ... .*
Um die Meinung zusammen zu fassen: *That's why ... . – To sum up, I would say ... .*

1 *Abschlussprüfung Englisch, Klasse 10, Cornelsen, 2003, Musterprüfung 2, Seite 21*
2 *Adapted from Wordmaster B5/6 zu English G 2000, Cornelsen, Seite 9*

Denke daran, dass du deine Meinung begründen musst, wenn dies gefordert wird *('Give reasons'.).*

Du möchtest das gleich einmal trainieren? Nun, dann schreibe z. B. deine Gedanken auf zu der Behauptung 'Boxing is a bloodsport!' Entscheide dich zuerst, ob du diese Ansicht teilst, oder ob du dem Boxsport gegenüber positiv eingestellt bist. Sammle dann Argumente für bzw. gegen das Boxen. Bringe diese Argumente in eine logische Reihenfolge und versuche Tatsachen und Beispiele zu finden, welche deine Meinung untermauern. Gehe erst danach an die schriftliche Ausarbeitung.

'What do you do or say?' ist eine weitere Aufgabenform, bei der du begründen sollst, wie du dich in einer bestimmten Situation verhalten würdest. Ein Beispiel aus dem Lehrbuch für Klasse 10: [1]

You and a friend have planned an evening together. He/She tells you that he/she has invited someone else to join you – someone you don't like.

Du könntest diese Übung auch mit einem Partner durchführen und einen Dialog erarbeiten:
Die Arbeitsaufgabe: "Write a dialogue which solves the conflict."

A: Excuse me, Sally. Have you got a minute?
B: Sure. What's up?
A: Well, I hate to say this, but ...

Im weiteren Verlauf des C-Teils musst du einen längeren Text verfassen. Oft lautet der entsprechende Hinweis: *"Write about 120 words."* Dabei kann es sich um ganz verschiedene Textsorten handeln, z. B. um eine Geschichte, eine Nacherzählung, einen Bericht, einen Brief usw. So könnte ein Zeitungsbericht beginnen: [2]

"A woman's handbag was stolen yesterday in Church Street. The old lady had just left a shop when ... "

Der Schluss des Zeitungsartikels lautet:

"... The young man brought the handbag back to the old lady."

Deine Aufgabe ist es, den fehlenden Teil des Zeitungsartikels zu ergänzen.

Write a letter.

Diese Aufgabenstellung kommt in schriftlichen Prüfungen sehr häufig vor. Auch wenn du sie eventuell ‚abwählen' kannst (siehe hierzu die Vorbemerkungen bezüglich des Teils C2), so solltest du wissen, wie ein formeller oder ein informeller Brief erstellt wird. Ein guter Weg, *'formal letters'* und *'informal letters'* von einander abzugrenzen, wird im Workbook zu English G 2000, Band B6 auf S. 11 aufgezeigt:

There are two letters mixed up here. One is a formal letter to a computer firm. The other is an informal one and not to a friend. Underline the sentences that are from the formal letter. Then write the letter out.

Dear Sir or Madam,
Hi Amy!
Thanks for your e-mail. It really made me laugh!
I am writing about a computer that I bought from your company.
I'm sending you this note because my stupid computer isn't working.
I have had a lot of problems with it and when I phoned your hotline, I did not get any help.
I am very unhappy with this situation, and I think your company should help me more.
I phoned the hotline, but they were useless. A strange voice told me to press lots of buttons.
I've written a letter to the company. I hope they answer it.

1 *English G 2000, Cornelsen 2001, Ausg. B, Band 6, S. 39*
2 *Nach EG 2000, Cornelsen 2000, Bd 5, S. 24*

I look forward to hearing from you.
I'll phone you at the weekend.
Lots of love,
Yours faithfully,
Mandy Hill
Mandy xxxx

Abschließend einige wichtige Hinweise zur Korrektur deiner selbst gestalteten Texte. Sie sind dem Lehrwerk English G 2000, Ausgabe B, Band 6, auf Seite 71 entnommen:

After you have written your text, take time to check it carefully. Go through the text several times; each time concentrate on something different, e.g.:

- *Check the **content.** Are all the ideas in it that you wanted? Does it make sense?*
- *Check the **grammar.** Pay special attention to tenses and word order.*
- *Check each word. Have you used the words correctly (e.g. the right prepositions with the verbs ...)? What about the spelling? (Here's a tip for checking the spelling: Read each word, one after the other, starting at the end of your text and going back to the beginning. Try it – it works!)*
- *Watch out for your **'favourite mistakes'.***
- *If you can, put the text away some time and do something completely different. Then read your text again. You may see it differently – the way another reader would. And you may find mistakes you didn't see before.*
- *If necessary, rewrite your text. Practise correcting with every text you write.*

Häufige Fehler (common mistakes)

'Nobody is perfect!' Dennoch – es lohnt sich aufzupassen, vor allem im C-Teil der Prüfungsaufgaben. Dort kannst du zwar viele Punkte erreichen, wenn du über einen guten und abwechslungsreichen Wortschatz verfügst. Es dürfen allerdings nicht zu viele grammatische Fehler in deinen von dir verfassten Texten vorkommen, sonst droht ein Punktabzug!

In den folgenden 18 Sätzen ist jeweils ***einer*** der in Klassenarbeiten und bei Abschlussprüfungen häufig vorkommenden Fehler versteckt. Vermutlich wirst du viele Fehler entdecken, aber kannst du sie auch berichtigen? Versuche es!

1. *It gives a lot of interesting sights in London.*
2. *I've known my friend Tim since many years.*
3. *Betty is taller as Mandy, but Peggy is the tallest.*
4. *We mustn't hurry – there is enough time.*
5. *We go often to the zoo – it's not far from here.*
6. *The most kids wear jeans at our school.*
7. *She worked hardly – so she earned a lot of money.*
8. *Do you sometimes the washing-up at home?*
9. *My brother plays basketball very good.*
10. *Listen, your mobile phone rings; don't use it here.*
11. *These informations are interesting.*
12. *Her sister is nurse at the hospital over there.*
13. *Bob often play football on Saturday afternoon.*
14. *He was bitten from a dog, but he's feeling better now.*
15. *If you would play with your brother, he would be happy.*
16. *She enjoys to speak French.*
17. *We're here in town since last Friday.*
18. *People which drive too fast in a village are careless.*

Solltest du Probleme haben, die richtigen Lösungen zu finden, kannst du die Regeln in einem Grammatikbuch nachschlagen. Dort wird dir zum Beispiel erklärt, weshalb im Satz 10 die Verlaufsform stehen muss. Wenn du die Kompaktausgabe der *'Cornelsen English Grammar'*[1] hast, kannst du im hinter der Lösung angegebenen Kapitel oder im Kapitel 20 ('common mistakes'), (S. 144 – 148) nachlesen. Auch im *'Practice Book'*[2] zur *'Cornelsen English Grammar'* findest du in Kapitel 20 (S. 149 – 150) ähnliche Übungen. In beiden Ausgaben werden weitere häufige Fehler aufgezeigt, berichtigt und besprochen.

D. Skills and Techniques

Der D-Teil der Abschlussprüfung umfasst in der Regel eine Übersetzung sowie eine Dolmetschübung bzw. eine Übung zur Weitergabe von Informationen.

Der Text, den du aus dem Englischen ins Deutsche zu übersetzen hast, wird in den meisten Fällen dem Ausgangstext auf Seite 1 der Abschlussprüfung entnommen. Dadurch ist er dir inhaltlich nicht mehr ganz fremd. In den vorhergehenden Teilen der schriftlichen Prüfung hast du dich bereits intensiv mit diesem Text als Ganzes befasst. Dennoch musst du beim Übersetzen einige wichtige Unterschiede im Gebrauch der beiden Sprachen beachten. Damit du das Übersetzen gleich ein bisschen üben kannst, werden die folgenden Hinweise teilweise auf Englisch gegeben:[3]

- *word order:*
  *They **often get** into trouble. (Sie **geraten oft** in Schwierigkeiten.)*
- *different use of nouns, verbs, adjectives and adverbs:*
  *He **loves** taking photos. (Er macht **liebend gern** Fotos.)*
- *prepositions:*
  *Going **to** museums can be fun. (Es kann Spaß machen, **in** Museen zu gehen)*
- *different ways of saying things mean you can't translate word for word:*
  *They dress **the same way**. (Sie ziehen sich **gleich** an.)*
- *different use of tenses:*
  *We **didn't** understand. (Wir **haben nicht** verstanden.)*

Zu jedem der oben genannten Punkte eine kleine Übersetzungsübung:

1. *Her brother came home **shortly before midnight yesterday.***
   (Beachte die unterschiedliche Satzstellung.)

2. *They **like** skiing. (Ändere die Wortart bei 'like'!)*

3. *I watched the match **on** TV. (Wähle eine andere Präposition.)*

4. *It **took her** five minutes **to get there**. (Übersetze nicht Wort für Wort.)*

5. ***We'll** do that later. (Verwende eine andere Zeitform.)*

In deinem Lehrbuch kannst du weitere Übungen zum Übersetzen finden, z. B. im bereits erwähnten Cornelsen-Lehrwerk English G 2000, Band 5 auf Seite 98 *('Skills Option19')* zur Übersetzung der im Englischen recht häufigen Partizipien.

1 *Cornelsen English Grammar, Kompaktausgabe, Cornelsen 2003, Best.-Nr. 63224*
2 *Practice book, Cornelsen Englisch Grammar, Kompaktausgabe, Cornelsen 2004, Best.-Nr. 371069*
3 *English G 2000, Cornelsen 2000, Band B5, S. 97*

E. Spelling Check

Wir haben bereits darauf hingewiesen, dass in der schriftlichen Abschlussprüfung deine Rechtschreibleistung bewertet wird. Darüber hinaus gibt es den Aufgabenteil E, bei dem es häufig darum geht, Rechtschreibfehler zu erkennen und zu berichtigen. Dies wird dir leichter fallen, wenn du ...

a) ... die wichtigsten Regeln zur Rechtschreibung kennst und diese anwenden kannst.
b) ... ein Gespür dafür bekommst, wo ein Rechtschreibfehler versteckt sein könnte.

Dieses ‚ein Gespür bekommen' kann man trainieren. Im folgenden Beispiel einer typischen Aufgabenstellung solltest du den Text genau durchlesen.

Übung 1: Im Bericht über *Sally Ride,* Amerikas erster Astronautin,[1] kommt in jedem der acht Sätze jeweils ***ein*** Rechtschreibfehler vor. Die Aufgabenstellung könnte lauten:

Check the sentences. Spot the spelling mistakes and correct them.

Lies die folgenden Tipps, bevor du versuchst, die Aufgabe zu lösen.

1. Der Text enthält drei Fehler, bei denen sich die englischen und die deutschen Wörter sehr ähneln. Dadurch übersieht man solche Fehler leicht.

2. In zwei Fällen muss statt einem *'y'* ein *'i'* bzw. ein *'ie'* stehen.

3. In einem der Sätze ist der Fehler schwer zu erkennen, weil das betreffende Wort einen ‚stummen' Laut enthält, der zwar nicht gesprochen, wohl aber geschrieben wird.

4. Du kennst wahrscheinlich die Regel, nach der das stumme *'e'* am Wortende bei der *-ing-Form* (meist) wegfällt. Dann findest du den diesen Fehler schnell!

5. Einen weiteren Fehler konnte nicht einmal das Korrekturprogramm des Computers entdecken. Es gibt nämlich zwei Wörter mit derselben Aussprache, von denen jedoch nur eines im betreffenden Satz einen Sinn ergibt. Solche Wörter werden im Englischen *'homophones'* genannt.

1. In 1977 Sally Ride had almost finished her time at Stanford University and begann to look for a job. 2. One day, while looking in the 'help wanted' section of the Stanford Daily, Sally saw a job add that would change her life. 3. NASA was looking for young scientists who wanted to become 'mission specalists'. 4. Sally applyed for the job. 5. In Oktober 1977 she flew to Lyndon B. Johnson Space Center outside Houston, Texas, for interviews. 6. Usually a cool person, Sally remembers having a few butterflys in her stomach during the interviews. 7. On the morning of January 16, 1978, Sally got a telefon call from NASA. 8. "Well, we've got a job here for you if you're still interested in takeing it."

Wichtige Rechtschreibregeln:

1. a) Bei der Pluralbildung von Nomen wird aus 'y' meist '-ies' (*family – families;* aber: *boy – boys!*).
   b) Bei einem Wort, das auf *'o'* endet, wird oft *'-es'* angehängt (*potato – potatoes;* aber: *radio – radios*!).
   c) Bei Nomen, die auf *'f'* oder *'fe'* enden, bildet man den Plural meist mit *'-ves'*.(*wife – wives;* aber: *roofs* („Dächer").
   d) Nach Zischlauten hängt man *'-es'* an (*bus – buses*).
   e) Bei den unregelmäßigen Pluralformen helfen Regeln nicht weiter. Man muss sich solche Nomen gut einprägen (z. B.: *foot – feet*).

1 *English G 2000, Band 5, S. 39*

Übung 2: *Complete the sentences with the nouns from the list in the plural.*[1]

child life party sandwich tomato woman

1. *I've made a salad – just cheese, lettuce, eggs and ... .*
2. *...of all ages like to play computer games.*
3. *Debbie likes to go out at the weekends. She goes to a lot of ... .*
4. *There was a train crash yesterday. Three passengers lost their ... .*
5. *Alan and Beth gave their seats to two old ... in the bus.*
6. *Mum has made some ... for our trip. They're in the fridge.*

2a) Schreibung der *-s-Form* bei Verben.

Es reicht nicht ganz aus, wenn du weißt, dass man in der dritten Person Singular des *'simple present'* ein *'-s'* anhängt. Du solltest auch die dabei eventuell notwendigen Veränderungen des Wortstammes beachten. Solltest du bei der folgenden kleinen Aufgabe ein Problem haben, dann schlage bitte in deinem Grammatikbuch nach (in der Kompaktausgabe der Cornelsen-Grammatik z. B. im Kap. 54 auf Seite 43).

Übung 3: *Write out the 3rd person singular simple present of the following verbs:*

1. finish 2. hurry 3. do 4. kiss 5. tidy 6. say 7. lose 8. watch

2b) Schreibung der -ing-Form

Gelegentlich wird ein einzelner Endkonsonant verdoppelt *(sit – sitting)*, oder es fällt das '-e' am Ende des Infinitivs weg *(phone – phoning)*.

Übung 4: *There are six spelling mistakes in the following list of -ing forms. Find them and spell the forms correctly.*[2]

dancing planing prefering lying comming stopping offerring running controling swiming hoping

Übung 5: *Now write down the -ing forms of these verbs:*[2]

fit travel lie promise hurry rise

2c) Schreibung der simple past-Form der regelmäßigen Verben.

Bei Verben, die auf einen Konsonanten + y enden, schreibt man *'-ied'*. Nach einem einzelnen, betonten Vokal wird ein einzelner Endkonsonant verdoppelt.

Übung 6: *Write down the simple past form of these verbs:*

rob plan tidy control hurry prefer

1 *Practice Book zur CEG, Kap. 12, S. 103*
2 *Practice Book zur CEG, Kap. 5, Spelling check 2, S. 43*

3. Homophone

Es handelt sich um Wörter gleicher Lautung, aber unterschiedlicher Schreibung und Bedeutung. Du könntest dir für Übungszwecke eine Liste derartiger Wortpaare anlegen. Dann kannst du entweder die linke oder die rechte Seite der jeweiligen Spalte abdecken und dich selbst testen, ob du den fehlenden Begriff schreiben kannst, etwa nach folgendem Muster:

allowed	aloud	hear	here	pair	pear
brake	break	hole	whole	scene	seen
buy	by	knew	new	son	sun
cause	course	meat	meet	steal	steel
for	four	one	won	wood	would

Es handelt sich hierbei nur um eine kleine Auswahl von 'homophones'. Suche selbst weitere Beispiele! Du findest solche u. a. in der abschließenden Übung.

Übung 7:

A hurricane hunter (a pilot who flies into the centre of a hurricane) talks about his job.
One *of the two missing words in each of the sentences below is given here:*

eye piece right bored whether there through wear

1. *Our job is interesting – I guess you will never get ... on ... of our plane.*
2. *We know exactly ... the life jackets are which we ... in case of emergency.*
3. *I think a journalist who has never taken a flight into a hurricane has no ... to ... about our job.*
4. *Sometimes ... are reporters on board who never put down ... cameras during the flight.*
5. *When ... got into the ... of a hurricane for the first time I was surprised how calm it was there.*
6. *One of the men ... off some instruments as soon as the aircraft got ... into the calm centre.*
7. *... the ... is terrible or not, it's our job to fly that plane – even under the worst conditions.*
8. *Let me give you a ... of advice: Please leave us in ... and don't ask too many questions!*

Und nun: Viel Erfolg bei der Schriftlichen Abschlussprüfung!

Anhang 1

Hier erhältst du eine Liste der Arbeitsanweisungen, die in Prüfungsaufgaben vorkommen. Wenn du eine Anweisung nicht verstehst oder ein Wort vergessen hast, kannst du hier nachschauen.

A-Teil:

Complete/finish the sentences with information from the text.	Ergänze die Sätze mit Informationen aus dem Text.
Answer the questions.	Beantworte die Fragen .
The answers needn't be in the text.	Die Antworten müssen nicht im Text stehen.
You do not have to write complete sentences.	Du brauchst keine vollständigen Sätze zu schreiben.
Decide whether the following statements are right or wrong.	Entscheide, ob die folgenden Aussagen richtig oder falsch sind.
Give advice.	Gib Ratschläge.
Ask questions.	Bilde Fragen.

B-Teil :

Explain the meaning of the words.	Erkläre die Bedeutung der Wörter.
Choose three of the following items and explain them in a complete sentence.	Wähle drei der folgenden Begriffe aus und erkläre in einem Satz, was diese bedeuten.
Name the things that are described here.	Benenne die hier beschriebenen Dinge.
Write complete sentences.	Schreibe vollständige Sätze.
Read the text and write down the suitable form of the words (given in brackets).	Lies den Text und schreibe die passende Form der (in Klammern angegebenen) Wörter.
Write down the correct prepositions.	Schreibe die richtigen Präpositionen auf .
Make new words.	Bilde neue Wörter.
Write down expressions from the text which mean more or less the same.	Schreibe Begriffe, die im Text vorkommen, und die praktisch dieselbe Bedeutung haben.
Find the corresponding nouns.	Suche/Finde die entsprechenden Hauptwörter.
Find the expression that is missing in each sentence below.	Suche/Finde den fehlenden Ausdruck in jedem der unten stehenden Sätze.
Which expressions match the definitions below?	Welche Begriffe passen zu den unten stehenden Worterklärungen?
Put the verbs into the correct tense.	Setze die Verben in die richtige Zeitform.

C-Teil:

Continue the dialogue.	Führe den Dialog weiter.
Give your opinion.	Lege deine Meinung dar.
What do you think of/about it?	Was denkst du darüber?
Write a possible ending of the story.	Schreibe ein mögliches Ende der Geschichte.
What do these signs here mean?	Was bedeuten diese Zeichen/Piktogramme?
What would you do or say?	Wie würdest du reagieren?
What would you suggest?	Was würdest du vorschlagen?
Make four suggestions.	Mache vier Vorschläge.
Write a a dialogue/a letter/a story.	Schreibe einen Brief/einen Dialog/eine Geschichte.
Explain yourself.	etwa: Erläutere, wie du reagieren würdest.
Give information.	Erteile Auskünfte.
Write sentences about your ideas.	Schreibe Sätze über deine Ideen/Vorstellungen.
Imagine ...	Stelle dir ... vor.

D-Teil:

Translate into German.	Übersetze ins Deutsche.
Report the meaning.	Gib die Bedeutung wieder.
Pass on/Transfer the information.	Gib die Informationen weiter.
Interpret ...	Dolmetsche ...

E-Teil:

Check the sentences.	Überprüfe die Sätze.
Spot the mistakes.	Entdecke die Fehler.
Correct the spelling mistakes.	Berichtige die Rechtschreibfehler.
Write down the plural forms of the nouns.	Bilde die Mehrzahl der Hauptwörter.
There is the same sound in all the words.	Alle Wörter enthalten den gleichen Laut.
Single or double letters?	Einfache oder doppele Buchstaben?
Find the missing letters.	Suche/Finde die fehlenden Buchstaben.
Add the correct ending.	Füge die richtige Endung des Wortes hinzu.
Write down the numbers in words.	Schreibe die Zahlen in Worten.
Make adjectives from the words.	Bilde Eigenschaftswörter aus den Wörtern.
Fill in the gaps with the correct words.	Ergänze die Lücken mit den richtigen Wörtern.
Which spelling is correct?	Welche Schreibweise ist richtig?

Further important instructions	Weitere wichtige Arbeitsanweisungen
Continue the dialogue.	Führe den Dialog weiter.
How do you say these things in English?	Wie sagt man diese Dinge auf Englisch?
Label the map.	Beschrifte die Karte.
Make a mind map.	Erstelle eine mind map.
Make a network.	Bilde ein Netzwerk (aus Begriffen).
Make new words.	Bilde neue Wörter.
Match the sentence halves.	Ordne die Satzhälften einander zu.
Put the words in the right order.	Bringe die Wörter in die richtige Reihenfolge.
Report the meaning.	Gib die Bedeutung wieder.
Use these notes.	Verwende diese Notizen.
What do you think of/about it?	Was denkst du darüber?
Which words go together?	Welche Wörter passen zueinander?
Write a possible ending.	Schreibe einen möglichen Schluss.
Write sentences about your ideas.	Schreibe Sätze über deine Ideen.

Teste dich selbst!

Bevor du an Aufgaben zur Schriftlichen Abschlussprüfung herangehst, kannst du dich selbst prüfen, ob deine Fähigkeiten, Fertigkeiten und Kenntnisse zu einer guten Leistung führen. Kreuze hinter den folgenden Sätzen an, was bei dir immer, oft oder selten zutrifft.

Aufgabenteil A (Textverständnis): Ich kann ...	*immer*	*häufig*	*selten*
... schon beim flüchtigen Lesen des Textes herausfinden, worum es geht.	☐	☐	☐
... wichtige Informationen, die der Text bietet, schnell erkennen.	☐	☐	☐
... nach dem genaueren Lesen darlegen, was der Textautor sagen will.	☐	☐	☐
... entscheiden, ob bestimmte Aussagen im Text richtig oder falsch sind.	☐	☐	☐
... Fragen, die zum Ausgangstext gestellt werden, beantworten.	☐	☐	☐
... selbst Fragen bilden, die mit dem Inhalt des Textes zu tun haben.	☐	☐	☐

Aufgabenteil B (Wortschatz und Grammatik): Ich kann ...	*immer*	*oft*	*selten*
... Wörter finden, die gleiche oder ähnliche Bedeutung wie andere haben.	☐	☐	☐
... kenne passende Wörter (z. B. das Hauptwort zu einem Zeitwort).	☐	☐	☐
... Wörter in einem Text ergänzen (z. B. Präpositionen wie *in*, *at*, *on*).	☐	☐	☐
... die Bedeutung von englischen Wörtern und Begriffen erklären.	☐	☐	☐
... erkennen, wann ein Adjektiv *(quick)* oder ein Adverb *(quickly)* steht.	☐	☐	☐
... Zeitformen richtig verwenden (steht 'simple past' oder 'present perfect'?)	☐	☐	☐

Aufgabenteil C (Erstellung von Texten): Ich kann ...	*immer*	*oft*	*selten*
... meine Meinung darlegen und sie begründen.	☐	☐	☐
... meine eigenen Gefühle und die meiner Mitmenschen beschreiben.	☐	☐	☐
... Vermutungen über einen Sachverhalt äußern.	☐	☐	☐
... Texte zusammenfassen, nacherzählen oder zu Ende schreiben.	☐	☐	☐
... Dialoge erfinden bzw. unvollständige Dialoge vervollständigen.	☐	☐	☐
... Briefe, Geschichten, Berichte, Zeitungsartikel u. ä. schreiben.	☐	☐	☐

Aufgabenteil D (Arbeitstechniken und Fertigkeiten): Ich kann ...	*immer*	*oft*	*selten*
... in Alltagssituationen die Aufgaben des Dolmetschers übernehmen.	☐	☐	☐
... die Rolle eines Interviewpartners übernehmen.	☐	☐	☐
... einem Text Informationen entnehmen und weitergeben.	☐	☐	☐
... einen deutschen Kommentar zu englischen Texten geben.	☐	☐	☐
... mit einem zweisprachigen Wörterbuch umgehen.	☐	☐	☐
... Texte aus dem Englischen ins Deutsche übersetzen.	☐	☐	☐

Aufgabenteil E (Rechtschreibung): Ich kann ...	*immer*	*oft*	*selten*
... in einem Text verborgene Rechtschreibfehler entdecken.	☐	☐	☐
... die Pluralformen von unregelmäßigen Hauptwörtern schreiben.	☐	☐	☐
... englische Zahlen schreiben (z. B. 40 = *forty*, nicht *fourty*!)	☐	☐	☐
... Wortendungen unterscheiden (z. B. *-ence/-ance* oder *-er/-or*)	☐	☐	☐
... die Regeln für die Verdoppelung von Mitlauten anwenden *(sit – sitting)*.	☐	☐	☐
... einen gesamten Test auf Rechtschreibfehler hin überprüfen.	☐	☐	☐

1 Global  Pizza

So you thought the hamburger was the world's most popular fast food? After all, McDonald's Golden Arches span the globe. But no, there is another truly universal fast food, the ultimate fast food. It's easy to make, easy to serve, much more varied than the hamburger, can be eaten with the hands, and it's delivered to your front door or served in fancy restaurants. It's been one of America's favourite foods for over 50 years. It is, of course, the pizza.

It's kind of silly to talk about the moment when pizza was 'invented'. It gradually evolved over the years, but one thing's for certain – it's been around for a very long time. The idea of using pieces of flat, round bread as plates came from the Greeks. They called them 'plakuntos' and ate them with various simple toppings such as oil, onions, and herbs. The Romans enjoyed eating something similar and called it 'picea'. By about 1000 A.D. in the city of Naples, 'picea' had become 'pizza' and people were experimenting with more toppings: cheese, ham, anchovies, and finally the tomato, brought to Italy from Mexico and Peru in the sixteenth century. Naples became the pizza capital of the world. In 1889, King Umberto I and Queen Margherita heard about pizza and asked to try it. They invited pizza maker Raffaele Esposito to make it for them. He decided to make the pizza like the Italian flag, so he used red tomatoes, white mozzarella cheese, and green basil leaves. The Queen loved it and the new pizza was named 'Pizza Margherita' in her honour.

Pizza migrated to America with the Italians at the end of the nineteenth century. The first pizzeria in the United States was opened in 1905 at 53 ½ Spring Street, New York City, by Gennaro Lombardi. But the popularity of pizza really exploded when American soldiers returned from Italy after World War II and raved about 'that great Italian dish'. Americans are now the greatest producers and consumers of pizza in the world.

(333 words)

Pizza Trivia

- *Americans eat 350 slices of pizza per second.*
- *There are 61,269 pizzerias in the United States.*
- *Pizza is a $30 billion per year industry.*
- *October is national pizza month in the United States.*
- *The world's first pizzeria, the Antica Pizzeria Port'Alba, which opened in Naples in 1830, is still alive.*
- *Pizza Hut has over 12,000 restaurants and takeaway outlets in over 90 countries.*
- *In America, pepperoni is the favourite topping.*
- *Anchovies is the least favourite.*
- *In Japan, eel and squid are favourites.*
- *In Russia, it's red herring, salmon and onions.*
- *In Brazil, they like green peas on their pizza.*
- *In Australia the favourites are shrimp and pineapple.*
- *The French love bacon and crème fraîche on theirs.*
- *The English love tuna and sweetcorn.*

4 ***fancy:*** *vornehm, schick*
7 ***to evolve:*** *(sich) entwickeln*
27 ***to migrate:*** *zuwandern, einwandern*
33 ***to rave:*** *schwärmen*
47 ***takeaway outlet:*** *Verkaufsstellen*
51 ***eel:*** *Aal*
51 ***squid:*** *Tintenfisch*

A. TEXT BASED TASKS *18 pts*

1 *Decide whether the following statements are right or wrong.* *4 pts*

	true	false
1. The pizza was invented when Italians emigrated to the USA.	☐	☐
2. More pizzas are eaten in the USA than anywhere else in the world.	☐	☐
3. The Americans have a seasonal pizza celebration every year.	☐	☐
4. The colours of the Italian flag were made after the famous red, white and green 'Pizza Margherita'.	☐	☐

2 *Find the information in the text. You don't have to write complete sentences.* *6 pts*

1. Why is pizza even more popular than hamburgers? (three items)

___

2. Who ate 'plakuntos' and 'picea'? (two items)

___

3. Why was Naples famous 400 years ago? (one item)

___

3 ***Ask questions.*** *8 pts*

Your English friend has just come back from a holiday camp in the USA. Write four questions to ask him about the food and the meals there. Use different question forms.

1

2

3

4

B. USE OF LANGUAGE 24 pts

1 Vocabulary – Grammar

Read the text and write down the words listed below in the correct form. 12 pts

Hi! My name's Dan. I'm eighteen and I'm a pizza ______1______ boy. It's a great job but it's very ______2______. I deliver pizzas and then ride back to the pizza shop to collect more about ten times in one evening! I'm used to all sorts of weather but I have to be ______3______ when it rains because the roads are ______4______ and ______5______. Most customers are very ______6______ but some are ______7______ because they take ages to find their purse. What I hate are dogs who bark at me ______8______ when I ring at the door. The part of the job I like ______9______ is ______10______ the names of all the roads. I ______11______ some very funny ones like Happy Street or Fish Bowl Lane up to now! When I finish work at about 11 pm, I'm ______12______! Guess what I have for dinner? Yes, a pizza!

1.	deliver	4.	slip	7.	annoy	10.	learn
2.	tired	5.	danger	8.	angry	11.	discover
3.	care	6.	friend	9.	good	12.	starve

2 *Write complete sentences to explain the meaning of three of the following phrases.* 9 pts

1. it's been around (line 8) ______
2. toppings (line 12) ______
3. in her honour (line 26) ______
4. century (line 28) ______

3 *Find the words in the text (see lines 6-13) that have more or less the same meaning.* 3 pts

1. step by step ______
2. different ______
3. nearly the same ______

C. CREATIVE WRITING 27 pts

1 ***What would you do or say?*** 9 pts

Choose ***two*** *of the situations and explain yourself. Write about 60 words altogether.*

1. On the bus you see a backpack on an empty seat.
2. A friend lends you a computer game. He wants it back and you can't find it.
3. You've been out with a friend and come home late. Your mother says you can't see any friends for the next two weeks.
4. You arrive at the stadium to play in a match and find you've forgotten your shorts.

2 *Choose task A* ***or*** *B. Write about 120 words.* 18 pts

A. Write a story on the topic of your choice using the following words. Find a suitable headline.

invented	became famous	the idea

B. Write a report.

You have visited a restaurant that has just opened up.
Give your impressions on food, service, atmosphere, prices, etc.

D. SKILLS AND TECHNIQUES 25 *pts*

1 ***Pass on the information.*** **13** *pts*

Im folgenden Text geht es um Gerichte, die in den USA sehr beliebt sind. Dein Freund, der kein Englisch spricht, hat zu diesem Thema die unten stehenden Fragen. Bitte beantworte Sie auf Deutsch.

Ask for a hamburger, a sandwich, a hotdog, spaghetti and pizza almost anywhere in the world and you'll be understood! But strangely, this global food isn't modern at all – in fact, all these dishes have been around for a long time. Where did they originate? Well, it's pretty clear where the hamburger came from – Hamburg, in Germany, of course! When German immigrants from that city settled in New York in the early 1800's they introduced their speciality – cooked minced beef – to the Americans. To make it easier to eat, it was put in a 'bun' and today the hamburger has become the most popular fast food. Just like the hotdog – a long hot sausage in a bread roll – which originated in Frankfurt. In German it was called a 'dachshund' sausage, but once it was taken to the USA by German immigrants, Americans found it easier to call it simply a 'hot dog'! (Find out more on the website www.theholidayspot.com/hotdog).

The sandwich was invented by the Earl of Sandwich (Sandwich = a town in the south of England) in the eighteenth century because it was a quick and easy meal to eat while he was busy gambling!

Pizza and spaghetti were introduced to the world by the Italians who have been making these dishes for centuries. 'Pizza' means 'little pie' in Italian' and spaghetti, 'little cords'. Like the Germans, it was Italian immigrants in the USA who introduced their traditional dishes to the Americans. In fact, 'spaghetti' is just one of the hundreds of shapes of 'pasta' – an Italian word meaning a mixture of flour and water. Find out all about pasta shapes (macaroni, vermicelli, etc) and what their names mean on the website www.ilovepasta.org/shapes.

And for more information and history about all the dishes above, visit the website www.what'scookingamerica.net and click on 'History of Favourite Foods'.

Fragen

1. Kannst du die Gerichte Hamburger und Hot Dog kurz beschreiben? (5 Punkte)
2. Wie kamen diese Gerichte in die USA? (2 Punkte)
3. Warum wird mit 'Sandwich' ein schnelles und einfach zuzubereitender Imbiss bezeichnet? (2 Punkte)
4. Wie kamen 'Pizza' und 'Spaghetti' in die USA und was bedeuten die beiden Wörter? (4 Punkte)

2 *Translate the following paragraph (lines 27 through 35, page 16) into German.* **12** *pts*

Pizza migrated to America with the Italians at the end of the nineteenth century. The first pizzeria in the United States was opened in 1905 at 53 1/2 Spring Street, New York City, by Gennaro Lombardi. But the popularity of pizza really exploded when American soldiers returned from Italy after World War II and raved about 'that great Italian dish'. Americans are now the greatest producers and consumers of pizza in the world.

E. SPELLING CHECK *6 pts*

1 *'ie' or 'ei'?* **6** *pts*

Complete the words in the sentences with the correct spelling.

1. The ***ch***___?___***f*** Indian was sitting on the ground smoking a pipe.
2. I'm my uncle's nephew and my sister is his ***n***___?___***ce***.
3. I ***rec***___?___***ved*** an enormous parcel on my birthday.
4. You've got a much bigger ***p***___?___***ce*** of cake than me!
5. We jumped up and down on our beds, trying to touch the ***c***___?___***ling***.
6. The ***th***___?___***f*** ran out of the shop and jumped into a waiting car.

2 The Clown Doctor

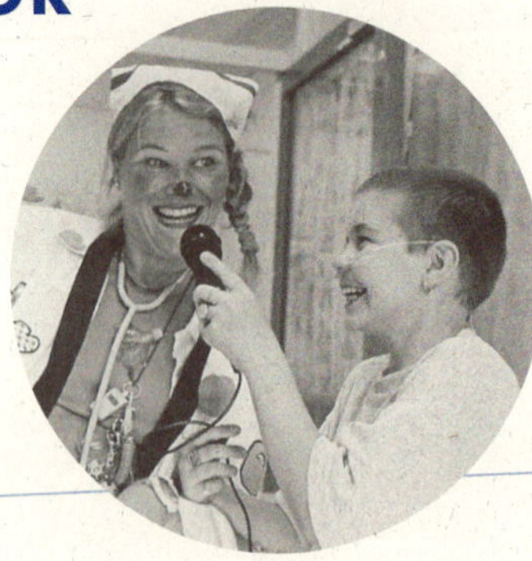

All over the world, children in hospital are being treated with a new kind of medicine: laughter. Lucy is 23 and works for the Theodora Children's Trust. She is one of many clown doctors who bring a smile to the faces of sick children.

"I'm a Theodora clown doctor. I call myself Dr. LooLoo. I spend two days a week in children's hospitals being extremely silly with my friend and colleague Dr. Chequers. We make funny faces, tell jokes, and do magic tricks. As I walk into the wards I blow bubbles, shake hands with the kids, and make up nonsense songs for those children well enough to sing. We take special balloons to make 'balloon animals' and tell funny stories about them. We often meet kids who one week look really sick, then we go back the next week and they're racing about yelling 'Hi there, Dr. LooLoo! Hi Dr. Chequers!'

I'm naturally a very cheerful person. I've always been a clown. In fact my father's a clown and I started working with him when I was eight years old. I knew it was just the job for me and I became a clown doctor because I think it's a great way to cheer up sick, frightened children in hospital. I wear a fancy coat, a yellow shirt, and tights with big stripes. Also, I have a red rubber nose and wear my hair in crazy plaits.

Being a clown in a hospital is very tiring both physically and emotionally. We have to learn not to show our feelings, otherwise we'd be useless. Clown doctors are sensitive but this is not a side most people see. To the children we're happy all the time. I'm still learning to allow myself to feel sad occasionally. There are special kids you get really close to. At the moment I'm working with a very sick little girl from Bosnia who speaks no English, so our only common language is laughter. She's been in and out of hospital for operations so many times and she's always on my mind.

At lunchtime we eat in the hospital cafeteria and that's really useful because we meet the nurses and doctors. They tell us about particular kids who they think will benefit from a clown doctor visit. If a child is frightened, perhaps they're being given an injection or some nasty medicine – we can distract them so the nurses can do their job.

At about six o'clock Dr Chequers and I take off our make-up and change our clothes. We're totally exhausted. Sometimes I have a night out with friends. It helps me unwind. When I finally fall into bed, I crash out. At weekends we are often asked to participate in events to raise money for the Theodora Children's Trust. It's a charity so we are paid with the money people give. Being a clown doctor makes the worries of everyday life seem small. All in all, I feel privileged to do this job."

(497 words)

14 ward: *Abteilung*
47 to benefit from: *Nutzen ziehen aus, profitieren von*
54 to unwind: *(sich) entspannen*
55 to crash out: *hier: abschalten, sofort einschlafen*

A. TEXT BASED TASKS 23 pts

1 *Finish the sentences using information from the text.* **6** *pts*

1. Lucy has always wanted to be a clown ever since ...

2. Clown doctors can't show their real feelings because ...

3. When a child is frightened or worried, Lucy ...

2 *Decide whether the following statements are right or wrong.* **3** *pts*

	true	false
1. Lucy spends every afternoon in the hospital.	☐	☐
2. Sometimes the children see that the clown doctor is sad.	☐	☐
3. It's important that the sick children understand English.	☐	☐
4. Lucy often talks about the sick children with the doctors and nurses.	☐	☐
5. Lucy and her colleague feel very tired at the end of the day.	☐	☐
6. At weekends the Children's Trust is never in Lucy's thoughts.	☐	☐

3 *Answer the questions in complete sentences. The answers needn't be in the text.* **9** *pts*

1. What kind of person do you think Lucy is?

2. How do sick children feel when they watch a clown doctor?

3. What do the clown doctors often do at the weekends?

4 ***Ask questions.*** **5** *pts*
You are interviewing Lucy, the clown doctor, about her work. Write five questions to ask her. Use at least three different question forms.

B. USE OF LANGUAGE *22 pts*

1 *Write sentences to explain the meaning of three of the following phrases.* ***9** pts*

1. to make a funny face (line 12)

____

2. to shake hands (line 14)

____

3. to cheer up sick children (lines 26-27)

____

4. to get close to someone (lines 37-38)

____

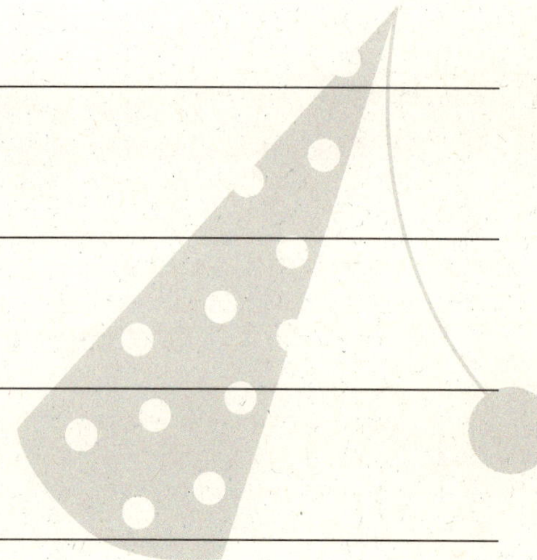

2 ***Vocabulary – Grammar***
Read the text. Find the suitable forms of the words and write them down. ***13** pts*

A Passage to India

When I _______1_______ university last year, I couldn't decide what sort of job I wanted to do so I decided to go abroad for a year. One of my friends had just come back from India, where he _______2_______ in a village school just outside Delhi. I was _______3_______ by his _______4_______ of India. He told me about the children who lived in such _______5_______ but were so happy to go to school. His stories _______6_______ me so much that I was _______7_______ persuaded to go there myself. My friend _______8_______ to the school and told them I was the _______9_______ teacher and I sent them a letter with my photograph. I got a summer job and saved up enough money for the plane fare. I flew to India at the _______10_______ of September. As I stepped out of the plane at Delhi Airport into the dust and the _______11_______, I remember _______12_______ very excited. This was the start of an _______13_______ adventure.

1.	leave	5.	poor	8.	write	11.	hot
2.	teach	6.	interest	9.	replace	12.	feel
3.	fascinate	7.	easy	10.	begin	13.	excite
4.	describe						

C. CREATIVE WRITING 27 pts

1 ***Describe a profession.*** *Write about 60 words.* **9** *pts*

The Theodora Children's Trust asked you to look for a person who would join the hospital as a clown doctor. Write a job description to appear as an advertisement in the local newspaper. Don't copy from the text.

2 *Choose task A **or** B. Write about 120 words.* **18** *pts*

A. Write a letter.

After a day at the hospital, Lucy, the clown doctor writes a letter to her friend, Anna, about one of the children she met.

B. Write an article to promote the Theodora Children's Trust.*

***to promote:** *werben für*

D. SKILLS AND TECHNIQUES 22 pts

1 *Interpret the interview.* 10 pts

You're in London with a friend who wants to find out about the Theodora Children's Trust. He's interviewing a spokesman who works for the Trust. Since your friend doesn't speak English very well you'll have to interpret his questions. Write down the questions in English and give the answers in German.

Q Was genau macht der 'Theodora Children's Trust'?

____

A It's an organisation that trains clown doctors and sends them to hospitals to cheer up sick children.

____

____

Q Und wie lange gibt es ihn schon?

____

A Over ten years. The very first clowns went to a big London Children's Hospital in 1994.

____

____

Q Was lernen die Clown Doctors während ihrer Ausbildung?

____

A They have medical training where they learn about hospital procedures, infections and how to deal with sick children. And artistic training teaches them mime, acting, juggling, balloon sculpting and all sorts of other ways to entertain children.

____

____

____

Q In wie vielen Krankenhäusern in Großbritannien kommen Clown Doctors zum Einsatz?

____

____

A There are clown doctors in about ten major British hospitals at the moment.

____

____

2 *Translate the following paragraph (lines 31 through 43, page 22) into German.* **12** *pts*

Being a clown in a hospital is very tiring both physically and emotionally. We have to learn not to show our feelings, otherwise we'd be useless. Clown doctors are sensitive but this is not a side most people see. To the children we're happy all the time. I'm still learning to allow myself to feel sad occasionally. There are special kids you get really close to. At the moment I'm working with a very sick little girl from Bosnia who speaks no English, so our only common language is laughter. She's been in and out of hospital for operations so many times and she's always on my mind.

____

____

____

____

____

____

E. SPELLING CHECK **6** *pts*

1 *Complete the sentences with the -ing form of the following verbs.* **3** *pts*

1. Oh, stop (quarrel) ____________________ you two!
2. I saw her (hurry) ____________________ down the road to the station.
3. The kettle is (boil) ____________________. Can you make the tea, please?
4. Look! Laura Smith's (win) ____________________!
5. What a terrible noise! What's (happen) ____________________?
6. I've lived in five different towns. Now I'm fed up with (change) ____________________ schools.

2 *Choose the correct word in these phrases.* **3** *pts*

1. Did you ***here/hear*** the good news?
2. You mustn't ***break/brake*** your promise.
3. What a ***waist/waste*** of time!
4. Foxes have long bushy ***tales/tails***.
5. Someone's coming up the ***stairs/stares***!
6. If people eat too much, they put on ***wait/weight***.

3 Surfing with Sharks

Great white sharks are famous for eating almost everything, and fishermen have found all sorts of things in their stomachs, from car tyres to cuckoo clocks. But experts say that great white and other large sharks are mostly fond of eating seals, sea lions and sea turtles. Many marine biologists think there may be an explanation why sharks attack surfers more often than they attack divers, swimmers or fishermen.

When surfers swim out to sea looking for a big wave, they move the surfboard over the water with their arms and legs. From below, where the sharks are, the surfers and their boards look similar to seals or sea turtles. Sharks don´t see very well, so they probably attack surfers by mistake. In fact, sharks almost never try to eat a surfer once they know that he or she is not their favourite food.

In October 2003, 13-year-old Bethany Hamilton learnt a very hard lesson about sharks. Bethany, a champion surfer, was surfing with friends in Hawaii when, suddenly, a shark attacked. The 4.6-metre tiger shark took off her left arm and bit her shoulder and board. Fortunately, Bethany´s friends acted fast and saved her life. Now, after a series of operations, she has gone back to surfing, she has been on TV and in magazines, and some people in Hollywood are making a film about her story.

Bethany Hamilton was very lucky, and her future looks bright. But the future of sharks may not be so bright. In 2003 more than 100 million sharks were killed because of cruel and irresponsible fishing practices. Of the 390 species of shark, eighteen species are considered seriously endangered, and this number is growing every year.

Surfing is becoming more and more popular all over the world: In the Canary Islands and California, in Australia and the Algarve, people are riding the waves. Experts say that surfers need to learn how to live with sharks, because we humans are really only visitors in the sharks' natural environment. The International Shark Attack File, an organisation that helps surfers and swimmers protect themselves from shark attacks, gives these tips:

! Never surf alone !
! Never surf at night or in dark waters !
! If you see a shark, stay calm and leave the area quickly and quietly !
! Always take a first aid kit with you when you go surfing !

If we learn to respect sharks, we'll be able to surf safely. *(454 words)*

A. TEXT BASED TASKS *18 pts*

1 *Decide if the following statements are right or wrong.* *2 pts*

	true	false
1. Sharks' eyesight is not good enough to distinguish shapes.	☐	☐
2. Sharks often eat rubbish.	☐	☐
3. Fishing practices are responsible for killing millions of sharks.	☐	☐
4. The number of surfers has gone down over the last few years.	☐	☐

2 *Find the information from the text. You don't have to write complete sentences.* *6 pts*

1. How many different types of shark exist?

___

2. Which organisation was set up to give surfers information about sharks?

___

3. What should you do if you are in the water and see a shark?

___

3 ***Ask questions.*** *10 pts*

You are a TV programme presenter and have invited Bethany Hamilton to talk about her shark attack. Ask her five questions about it. Use at least three different questions forms.

___

___

___

___

___

B. USE OF LANGUAGE *24 pts*

1 *Vocabulary – Grammar*

Complete the text with the correct form of the words. *12 pts*

Panbanisha looks like an ordinary chimpanzee but, in fact, she is a chimp with a ______1______! She's unique because ______2______ have trained her to speak English! She doesn't actually speak – she types words onto the computer and the computer voice ______3______ speaks them. Her computer has a ______4______ designed keyboard and each key is ______5______ with a symbol which represents words such as 'apple', 'hot', 'tired'. Panbanisha has learnt 5,000 English words so when she's ______6______ she can say to her ______7______ 'Please get me a sandwich' and if she's ______8______ she says, 'Lemonade, please'. At first her trainers were ______9______ that she would confuse words and would be not be able to say anything. But she has an excellent memory and can express ______10______ very well. One hot day last summer, for example, after Panbanisha ______11______ the coins she had been given as a reward for learning new words, she said in sign language, 'I'm ______12______! Please buy me a pool. The money's in my purse.'

1.	different	4.	special	7.	keep	10.	oneself
2.	science	5.	mark	8.	thirst	11.	save
3.	automatic	6.	hunger	9.	worry	12.	boil

2 *Write complete sentences to explain the meaning of three of the following phrases.* *9 pts*

1. car tyres (line 3)
2. a series of operations (line 24)
3. fishing practices (line 36)
4. a first aid kit (line 53)

3 *Find the words in the text which mean the opposite of the words below. The corresponding paragraph is indicated in the brackets.* *3 pts*

1. above (lines 10 – 17)
2. easy (lines 18 – 27)
3. humane (lines 28 – 39)

C. CREATIVE WRITING 27 pts

1 ***What would you do or say?***
Choose **two** *of the following situations and explain yourself. Write about 60 words altogether.* 9 pts

1. You're standing on the beach and you see someone in difficulty in the sea.

2. You spent all evening learning a page of your Geography book for a test next day. In the morning you realize you have been studying the wrong page.

3. You've forgotten your key and nobody's at home.

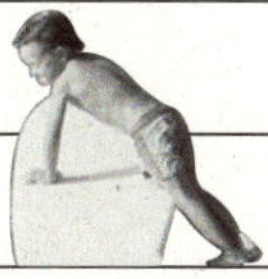

2 *Choose tasks A* ***or*** *B.*
Do not work on both tasks. Write about 120 words. 18 pts

A. Write a letter

You went for a holiday in Hawaii and stayed in a holiday sports club. You spent most days learning to surf and watching the other surfers riding the waves. Write a letter to a friend back home describing one particular day.

B. Write a story
Write a story using the following words:

wallet	address	reward

Start like this: I was walking to my friend's house the other day when I saw ...
and finish up like this: Ten pounds! More than a month's pocket money!

D. SKILLS AND TECHNIQUES 25 pts

1 *Transfer the information.* 13 pts

Deine Freundin / dein Freund interessiert sich für den Surfsport. Sie / er versteht den Text nicht so gut und bittet dich daher, die folgenden Fragen zu den Informationen aus dem Internet auf Deutsch zu beantworten.

1. Du hast gesagt, dass hier etwas über den Ursprung des Surfens steht. Kannst du mir das bitte genauer erklären? (6 Punkte)
2. Was hat Captain Cook mit dem Surfsport zu tun? (2 Punkte)
3. Was ist ein 'Luau', und was spielt sich dabei ab? (5 Punkte)

Today surfing is an international sport and there are major surfing events all over the world in countries which have ocean coastlines and high waves – e.g. South Africa, Australia, California, Indonesia, the French Atlantic Coast and many other places. But how did surfing start? Many people believe it started in Hawaii – a tiny island chain in the Pacific Ocean. Centuries ago, 'riding the waves' was the traditional pastime of the local fishermen who sat or stood on boats shaped like long wooden boards. Great importance and power were given to skilful wave riders and only the élite were allowed to surf along the best shores. When Captain Cook discovered Hawaii in 1778, he recorded seeing the native Hawaiians surf-riding and was impressed by their skill. In 1959, the island officially became the last state of the United States of America and the American way of life has now taken over. However, some Hawaiian traditions still remain. One of them, of course, is surfing and Hawaii is considered to be the best place in the world to 'catch a wave'. And when the surfing's finished for the day, surfers can indulge in another Hawaiian tradition, the Luau; a celebration of feasting and dancing with traditional food like roasted pig and sweet potatoes, and the traditional drink called 'Mai Tai'. Every guest is given a garland of flowers or shells and the women and girls dance in the traditional way.

2 *Translate lines 10 through 17 (page 28) into German.* **12** *pts*

When surfers swim out to sea looking for a big wave, they move the surfboard over the water with their arms and legs. From below, where the sharks are, the surfers and their boards look similar to seals or sea turtles. Sharks don´t see very well, so they probably attack surfers by mistake. In fact, sharks almost never try to eat a surfer once they know that he or she is not their favourite food.

E. SPELLING CHECK *6 pts*

1 *There are six incorrect plural forms in the following text.* **6** *pts*

Unkind Nature

It was lovely warm spring weather last weekend so the Kents went out for the day with their two children, Anna and Theo. They wanted to get away from the busy streets in their town and the noise of the buses and lorrys so they drove into the country. The leafs on the trees rustled in the breeze and the sun shone down on the rooves of the houses as they drove through the villages. They parked their car near fields of cows with their young calfs and woolly sheep with their little lambs. As they walked down to the river to have their picnic, little Anna picked flowers and Theo chased butterflies. But sadly the day didn't end well for them. Anna paddled in the water and cut her feet on the sharp stones. And while Theo was eating some strawberries and peachs he was bitten by some mosquitos and soon he was covered in itchy red spots!

Now write the correct spelling.

1. ______________________
2. ______________________
3. ______________________
4. ______________________
5. ______________________
6. ______________________

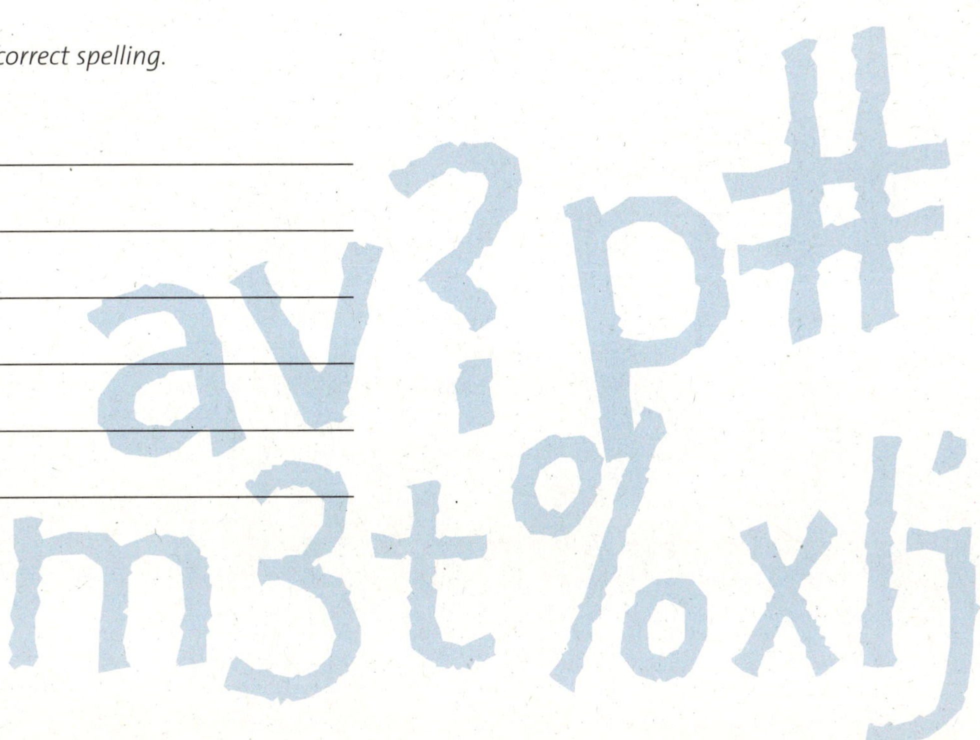

4 EARTH DAY

Imagine a day when 500 million people from 184 countries around the world come together to celebrate and protest with a single purpose in mind. This is just what happened on April 22nd, 2000. The day was Earth Day, and the purpose that the people had in mind was to work for a healthier and safer world for everyone. It was the biggest celebration of its kind in human history.

But April 22nd, 2000 was not the first Earth Day. In fact, it was the 30th anniversary of the first Earth Day celebration. In 1962, Gaylord Nelson, a US Senator, looked at the world around him and saw lakes and rivers polluted by rubbish and chemicals, forests that were slowly being destroyed every day, and towns and cities full of smog and car exhaust. Senator Nelson felt that the Government was not doing nearly enough to protect the environment. So he spent the next eight years travelling round the USA and talking to all sorts of people about pollution and other dangers that were harming the planet.

Finally, on April 22nd, 1970, Senator Nelson and a group of university students organized the first Earth Day. The event was much more successful than the organizers had ever expected: over 20 million people – young and old, rich and poor, city people and country people – took part.

Today, Earth Day is celebrated all over the world, and some countries even celebrate Earth Week the week before April 22nd, and Earth Month throughout the whole month of April. Over 5,000 different environmental organizations are connected by the Internet, and they help people in their communities to plan demonstrations, campaigns, talks and other activities. But the idea is the same as it was in 1970: the millions of people from all over the planet, rich and poor, old and young, who want to build a healthier and safer world.

The problems that Gaylord Nelson saw everywhere in the 1960s still exist, and now we know about things like global warming and acid rain that most people could not even imagine 40 years ago. We need Earth Day today more than ever. So what can we do? Many young people participate through their schools on Earth Day. They organize clean-up campaigns or pick up rubbish in their communities. Others write letters to their Council asking for more environmental protection laws. Still others organize marches to promote recycling and other energy-saving activities. But perhaps the best way to celebrate Earth Day is to follow the organizers' advice: "Do something nice for the Earth, have fun, meet new people, and make a difference."

(442 words)

A. TEXT BASED TASKS *24 pts*

1 *Match the two halves of the sentences.* *5 pts*

1. A politician and some students
2. The problems Senator Nelson saw almost 50 years ago
3. Today there is more pollution
4. Earth Day is
5. The first Earth Day brought together

A. are still there
B. a big international meeting
C. organized the first Earth Day
D. than in 1962
E. millions of people

1 ☐ 2 ☐ 3 ☐ 4 ☐ 5 ☐

2 *Find the information in the text. You don't have to write complete sentences.* *11 pts*

1. What is the purpose of Earth Day? (1 item)

___

2. What different kinds of pollution did Senator Nelson see? (3 items)

___

3. What do environmental organizations help people do? (4 items)

___

4. How can school-children fight against pollution? (3 items)

___

3 ***Ask questions.*** *8 pts*

A friend calls you on your mobile phone. He's in the street, taking part in a local Earth Day march in your town and he asks you to join him. You want to get some more information. Ask him four questions, using different question forms.

___

___

___

___

B. USE OF LANGUAGE *21 pts*

1 *Vocabulary – Grammar*

Complete the text with the correct form of the words. **12** *pts*

The North Yorkshire Moors in England is one of the ____1____ parts of Britain. It is a ____2____ beautiful region and many people come here for a walking or hiking holiday because it's so ____3____ and ____4____. The scenery is ____5____ and you can see wildlife such as deer and eagles. There is a big choice of ____6____ activities to do such as hang gliding, rock climbing and pony trekking. For walkers, it's important to wear strong walking shoes because the ground can be ____7____. The Moors cover a very big area and you can spend all day walking without seeing anyone. So a compass and a map are very ____8____ in case you get ____9____! Throughout the Moors there are small ____10____ villages with simple but ____11____ inns and hostels where hikers can stay overnight and have a big healthy breakfast before ____12____ again.

1. wild	4. relax	7. rock	10. tradition
2. particular	5. impress	8. use	11. comfort
3. peace	6. excite	9. lose	12. set off

2

Write complete sentences to explain the meaning of two of the following words. **6** *pts*

1. celebration (line 7)

____

2. rubbish (line 13)

____

3. environment (line 17)

____

3

Find the words in the text that have more or less the same meaning. **3** *pts*
The corresponding paragraph is indicated in brackets.

1. the aim (lines 1 – 8) ______________________________
2. during (lines 27 – 37) ______________________________
3. take part (lines 38 – 52) ______________________________

C. CREATIVE WRITING *27 pts*

1 ***What would you do or say?*** *9 pts*

Choose **two** *of the situations and explain yourself. Write 60 words altogether.*

1. During a lesson about the environment, your teacher asks you to suggest ways to help reduce wasting water and paper.
2. In your local shop, you see a girl take a packet of chewing gum and put it in her pocket without paying.
3. You live in a town on the coast. A tanker at sea has spilt oil and it has reached the town beach.
4. You arrive at school ten minutes late this morning. The teacher asks you why.

2 *Choose task A* ***or*** *B.* *18 pts*

Do not work on both tasks. Write about 120 words.

A. Write a report.

You are part of a school committee of pupils . Your task is to go round your school building and playground to inspect them for damage and rubbish. Write a report on what you did and what you found for the school magazine.

B Write a story.

Start like this:
The noise got louder and louder. I was intrigued* so I got up and went over to the window. I parted* the curtains and looked out. I saw the strangest thing!

* ***to be intrigued:*** *neugierig gemacht werden* * ***to part:*** *hier: öffnen*

D. SKILLS AND TECHNIQUES 22 pts

1 ***Pass on the information.*** 10 *pts*

Ein britischer Umweltexperte hat an deiner Schule einen Vortrag zum Thema "dein Beitrag gegen die Verschmutzung" gehalten. Was wurde über die fünf unten stehenden Fragen ausgesagt?

"You may think that you can't do much to help protect the environment. That it's too complicated and you need a lot of money. And maybe you feel that young people aren't really concerned. After all, it's adults who drive cars, work in factories, buy petrol and cut down trees. But, you're wrong. It's young people like you who can do an enormous amount to protect the environment by simply talking about it and being environment-friendly yourselves! There are lots of small ways you can help directly. If you start now, hopefully you'll continue the good habits as you get older. And it won't cost you a cent! For example, you can reduce the amount of traffic fumes simply by walking or cycling and not relying on parents to give you lift. And when you get a car of your own, organize car-sharing with your friends and neighbours. One car with four people in it is better than four cars with one person in it! Persuade your Mum not to use the car all the time for shopping, to get it all done in one trip and walk to local shops more often. And, talking of shopping, don't use plastic bags to bring it all home! Imagine the millions of bags being manufactured in factories – factories which contribute to air pollution and bags which take years to disappear. It's much better – and just as easy – to take your own shopping basket! And, by the way, check the labels on the things you buy and reduce chemical products to the minimum.

I'm sure you can think of lots of ways in your everyday life at home and at school to protect the environment: reducing pollution, saving precious water, and respecting the countryside and wild animals. It is essential to maintain the delicate balance of nature because without that balance, the environment is destroyed. And, don't forget, we human beings are part of that environment!

Fragen

1. Wie können junge Leute die Erwachsenen in ihrem Umweltverhalten beeinflussen?
2. Kannst du ein paar Beispiele geben, wie man Verkehrsabgase reduzieren kann?
3. Warum ist es besser, keine Plastiktüten zu verwenden?
4. Wie können wir sicherstellen, dass die von uns gekauften Produkte umweltverträglich sind?
5. Warum ist die Natur für uns Menschen so wichtig?

2 *Translate the following paragraph (lines 1 through 8, page 34) into German.* 12 *pts*

Imagine a day when 500 million people from 184 countries around the world come together to celebrate and protest with a single purpose in mind. This is just what happened on April 22nd, 2000. The day was Earth Day, and the purpose that the people had in mind was to work for a healthier and safer world for everyone. It was the biggest celebration of its kind in human history.

E. SPELLING CHECK 6 pts

1 *Correct the word which is spelt incorrectly in these sentences.* 6 pts

1. I'm exhausted! My tire burst so I had to walk most of the way.

   ____

2. She keeps her dairy in a locked box in the cupboard.

   ____

3. It is strictly forbiden to climb over the fence into the field.

   ____

4. For fried eggs, put a little oil in the pan and brake two eggs into it.

   ____

5. They've just built an enormous twenty-story office block in the centre of town.

   ____

6. I'll lend you my camera if you swear not to loose it!

   ____

5 Sailing Teens

When Seb Clover was just twelve years old, he already knew more about sailing than most adults. His father, Ian, who is a sailing instructor at the Isle of Wight UK Sailing Academy, had taught him all about yachts and sailboats.

One day, Seb's mum said to him and his father, "You two are so competitive! Why don't you have a race to see who is the best yachtsman?" She was only joking, but Seb and Ian took the idea very seriously. For the next three years, Seb spent every free moment training with his dad, and on December 19th, 2002, Seb set sail from Tenerife, Spain, on the greatest adventure of his life: a race across the Atlantic Ocean against his father.

Seb and Ian sailed alone aboard identical 9.8-metre Contessa yachts, so that neither would have an advantage. It took them three weeks to reach English Harbour, Antigua. In the end, Seb lost the race but, at the age of 15, he became the youngest person ever to cross the Atlantic on a solo voyage.

"The highlights were definitely seeing whales and dolphins... and especially reaching Antigua," says Seb. The worst moment was when he ran out of chocolate half-way through the 4,345-kilometre-voyage.

Of course, not everyone can enter the record books like Seb Clover. But every day there are more and more ways for teens to enjoy sailing. Student Ben East took part in the Round Britain Challenge 2003, a non-stop race round Britain and Ireland. "Life was at the best of times 'interesting' and, at the worst, almost impossible," says Ben, who spent twelve days on a 22-metre yacht with 17 other amateur yachtsmen and two professional seamen. Ben was the youngest crew member, and says of the experience, "It gave me the confidence to express my thoughts and be counted as a team member."

Another option for teens is sailing camp. For around 4,000 Euros, companies like Quest Voyages and Oddysey Expeditions offer teens between the ages of 13 and 19 the chance to earn sailing and scuba diving certificates while exploring the waters and islands of the Mediterranean, the Caribbean or Australia. Giorgina de Limon from Brussels says of her three-week-long adventure: "The best parts of the programme were the diving and sailing. The instructors were really good and the equipment was the best you could get." Catherine Leahy from Toulouse explains: "I learnt so much during those three weeks, from scuba diving to sailing to living with others. It was a fantastic trip."

It is no wonder then that yacht clubs around the world report that their members are getting younger and younger. Every day there are more sailing teens like Seb, Ben, Giorgina and Catherine.

(452 words)

A. TEXT BASED TASKS *19 pts*

1 *Correct the following statements.* *3 pts*
You need not write the complete sentence again – just correct the false words or phrases.

1. Ian's father is a swimming instructor.
2. Seb didn't like to spend his free time with his Dad.
3. Seb spent very little time training for the race against his father.
4. The boats that Seb and his father sailed were very different.
5. Seb and his Dad sailed from the Isle of Wight to Antigua.
6. It was Seb who won the race.

2 ***Who is who?*** *6 pts*
There are four teenagers mentioned in the text. (Seb, Ben, Giorgina and Catherine)
Write down the name of the person described in these sentences.

1. ? went sailing with seamen who were all older.
2. ? crossed the Atlantic single-handed.
3. ? found the equipment very good.
4. ? learnt three important things while on a sailing trip.
5. ? sailed around the British Isles.
6. ? was impressed by the instructors.

3 ***Ask questions.*** *10 pts*
You're interviewing Seb about his race across the Atlantic Ocean. Write five questions to ask him.
Use at least three different question forms.

1
2
3
4
5

B. USE OF LANGUAGE *20 pts*

1 *Complete these sentences by changing the nouns in brackets into their adjective form.* *6 pts*

1. I was ____________________ that we would win the race! (confidence)
2. Only very ____________________ yachtsmen sail single-handed. (experience)
3. 'The Vendée Globe' is a very difficult and ____________________ race. (challenge)
4. He has always been a ____________________ and fearless sailor. (courage)
5. If you really want to win you need to have a ____________________ spirit. (competition)
6. Living on the coast is very ____________________ if you're interested in sailing. (convenience)

2 *Find words or phrases in the text which have more or less the same meaning.* *6 pts*

1. to start a journey at sea (lines 6 – 14) ____________________
2. on a boat (lines 15 – 20) ____________________
3. a long journey alone across the ocean (lines 15 – 20) ____________________
4. to say what you think (lines 26 – 37) ____________________
5. the opportunity (lines 38 – 54) ____________________
6. It is not surprising. (lines 55 – 61) ____________________

3 *Find an incorrect word in each sentence and write down the correct word.* **8** *pts*

Learn to be a sailor!

1. Are you interested by sailing? ____________________
2. Come in Weston-on-Sea's Sailing Club and find out more. ____________________
3. We offer sailing classes to children from eight until sixteen. ____________________
4. There are courses all days of the week except Sunday. ____________________
5. You can choose a morning or afternoon class according at your level. ____________________
6. Each our instructors are NSF qualified. ____________________
7. Lessons are hold in our Club boats in Weston Bay. ____________________
8. Participants will receive a National Sailing Federation certificate in the end of the course. ____________________

C. CREATIVE WRITING *27 pts*

1 *Give your opinion on* **two** *of the following statements. Write about 60 words altogether.* **9** *pts*

1. Sailing is a sport for rich people.
2. Sailing isn't really a sport – it is just a leisure activity.
3. Sailing is a very dangerous sport.

2 *Choose task A* ***or*** *B.* **18** *pts*

A. *Write a letter and describe the following. Write about 120 words.*

You've just come back from a holiday camp for young people at the seaside. Write a letter to your British friend and tell him about the activities there.

B. *Write a story about a dangerous situation at sea. Use the following expressions in your text.*

yacht

terrible storm

rescue

D. SKILLS AND TECHNIQUES 22 pts

1 *Pass on the Information.* 10 pts

Unten stehend findest du einen Artikel über die bekannte britische Seglerin Ellen MacArthur. Dein Freund, der kein Englisch versteht, hat fünf Fragen zu Ellens Biografie, die du auf Deutsch beantworten sollst.

Imagine spending months alone on the ocean, sleeping in 20-minute intervals and lifting equipment far heavier than you are. This is the life and passion of the British yachtswoman, Ellen MacArthur. Ellen won the famous Vendée Globe Race in 2004 and became the fastest woman sailor and the youngest Briton to sail around the world non-stop.

How did Ellen become a champion? Ironically she grew up in the middle of England a long way from the sea. Her passion for sailing began when her aunt took her on a boat trip when she was 8. From that moment on, she was hooked! She read every sailing book she could find and took part in local sailing club races. By saving up her pocket money for 3 years and with help from her Granny, she bought her first boat. At 18, she sailed single-handedly around Britain and won the Young Sailor of the Year Award. She then started to take part in international races, improving her performance each time and was awarded the title Yachtsman of the Year.

But her major achievement was the Vendée Globe Race. Many people believed she was too young at 25, and too small at only 1.55m in height. Would she have the strength to sail alone for three months, make repairs, sail through storms, avoid icebergs, fight extreme tiredness and, all the while, keep sailing on course? Well, she did. And when she sailed through the finishing line in Britanny, Northern France, there were 20,000 people waiting to greet her.

"I'm lucky to be doing what I love", she says. She believes in sharing her luck. In her cabin there's a photo of a little girl smiling. She is one of a group of children with cancer whom Ellen takes on sailing trips. "Those kids have big problems but they keep smiling", she says. "When I'm at sea facing problems, I think of those smiles and it keeps me going". (325 words)

9 ***to be hooked:*** *sich für etwas begeistern, Feuer und Flamme sein.*

Fragen

1. Wo ist Ellen aufgewachsen und wie kam sie zum Segeln?
2. Wie konnte sie sich ihr erstes Boot leisten?
3. Welche Preise hat Ellen gewonnen?
4. Welchen Herausforderungen musste sie sich während des Vendée-Globe Rennens stellen?
5. Auf welche Weise lässt Ellen andere Menschen an ihrer Leidenschaft fürs den Segelsport teilhaben?

2 *Translate the following paragraph (lines 6 through 14, page 40) into German.* **22** *pts*

One day, Seb's mum said to him and his father, "You two are so competitive! Why don't you have a race to see who is the best yachtsman?" She was only joking, but Seb and Ian took the idea very seriously. For the next three years, Seb spent every free moment training with his dad, and on December 19th, 2002, Seb set sail from Tenerife, Spain, on the greatest adventure of his life: a race across the Atlantic Ocean against his father.

E. SPELLING CHECK 12 *pts*

1 *Many sporting activities in English end with 'ing'. E.g. to sail: sailing* **6** *pts*
Change the verbs into sporting activities.

1. to cycle ______________________________

2. to canoe ______________________________

3. to run ______________________________

4. to skate ______________________________

5. to ski ______________________________

6. to swim ______________________________

2 ***Suffixes: sion / ssion / cian / tion*** **6** *pts*
Add the correct suffix to the following letters to complete the words.

1. explana ______________________________

2. expre ______________________________

3. politi ______________________________

4. direc ______________________________

5. explo ______________________________

6. electri ______________________________

6 One Who Understands

When Matt Kelley was growing up in the United States, he often thought to himself, "Who am I?". Of course, there is nothing unusual about this; most teenagers ask themselves the same question from time to time. But Matt's problem was special. When he saw his schoolmates, he didn't see anyone who looked like him. There were white kids and black kids, Asian kids and Hispanic kids, but none like him. And when Matt went home and switched on the TV or opened a magazine, he still didn't see anyone who was quite like him.

Matt Kelley was a multiracial teen: his dad was white and his mum was Korean. He felt that he didn't quite fit in with white kids because of his Asian side, and that he didn't quite fit in with Asians because he was half white. This made him feel confused and frustrated, and he often wondered if he was the only teenager in the world with this problem.

In Matt's first year at university, he met other multiracial young people, and he began to talk with them about the problems that they had in common. He soon realized that there were lots of multiracial people in the U.S. and that they didn't really have a place to discuss their experiences. So in 1998, when Matt was only 19, he founded MAVIN. MAVIN, which means "one who understands" in Hebrew, is a magazine for young multiracial people who want to read about other people of mixed race and their experiences. It publishes articles about the unique problems that affect multiracial teens and invites its readers to write their own stories for publication in the magazine.

In a recent survey, when a group of American teens were asked if they had ever dated someone of a different race or ethnic background, 60% said yes. This, and the popularity of multiracial celebrities like Tiger Woods, Halle Berry, Lenny Kravitz and Mariah Carey, has made people reconsider the old concepts of race. " Multiracial means disregarding old models," explains Matt Kelley. "It means there are no boundaries to race. We can be comfortable being whatever we want to be."

Today, in addition to editing his magazine, Matt is president of the MAVIN Foundation, an organisation that gives support to multiracial teens and their families. He is truly "one who understands."

(396 words)

26 *Hebrew:* *Hebräisch*
36 *celebrities:* *Berühmtheiten*

A. TEXT BASED TASKS *24 pts*

1 *Finish these sentences using information from the text.* *5 pts*

1. Matt's problem was that ________________
2. Matt discovered that there were a lot of multiracial people when ________________
3. Matt's magazine MAVIN is for ________________
4. The magazine articles are about ________________
5. The MAVIN Foundation is an organization which ________________

2 *Find the information in the text. You don't have to write complete sentences.* *9 pts*

1. What kind of kids did he go to school with? ________________
2. Why is Matt described as multiracial? ________________
3. What are MAVIN readers encouraged to do? ________________

3 ***Ask questions.*** *10 pts*

A survey for young people.

Your school magazine has published some questions to find out about German young people's attitudes to racial differences. A school magazine in a British school is planning to do a similar project about British young people. They have asked you to give them the list of questions you have prepared – in English, of course! Write down five questions from your list.

1 Do you ~~learn~~ know any black kids in our school?
2
3
4
5

B. USE OF LANGUAGE 20 *pts*

1 ***Prefixes: il / dis / un / im*** 6 *pts*

Add the correct prefix to the words in bold and rewrite the sentences correctly.
Example: ***to disregard*** *(line 39) – to have no regard for something (to consider it has no importance)*

1. I'm sorry but I don't ***agree*** with your idea. ______________________
2. Keep still! Do be ***patient***! ______________________
3. Our new neighbour isn't very ***friendly***. ______________________
4. In Sweden it isn't ***legal*** for parents to slap their children. ______________________
5. I don't ***like*** cleaning and tidying up my room. ______________________
6. In Japan it isn't ***polite*** to wear your shoes in the house. ______________________

2 *Explain the meaning of three of the following words and phrases from the text.* 8 *pts*

1. fit in (lines 12 – 18) ______________________
2. he wondered (lines 12 – 18) ______________________
3. problems ... in common (lines 19 – 32) ______________________
4. background (lines 33 – 42) ______________________

3 *Find the word or words in the text that have the same or almost the same meaning.* 6 *pts*
The corresponding paragraph is indicated in brackets.

1. young people between 13 and 19 years of age (lines 1 – 11) ______________________
2. puzzled (lines 12 – 18) ______________________
3. he found out (lines 19 – 32) ______________________
4. he created (lines 19 – 32) ______________________
5. went out with (lines 33 – 42) ______________________
6. well-known stars in entertainment and sport (lines 33 – 42) ______________________

C. CREATIVE WRITING 28 pts

1 *What would you do?* 10 pts

Choose **two** *of the following situations and explain yourself. Write about 60 words altogether.*

1. You're buying a ticket at the cinema and realize you have forgotten your student card which gives you a 50% reduction.

2. There's a new Asian pupil in your class. She's finding it difficult to understand the lesson.

3. You see a classmate bullying a multiracial pupil at your school.

____

____

____

____

____

____

____

2 *Choose task A* ***or*** *B.* 18 pts

Do not work on both tasks. Write about 120 words.

A. Write a story.

Here is a line from the ***middle*** of a story.
'Just then, the head teacher walked in. I was so embarrassed.'
Write the beginning and the end of the story.

B. Write a letter.

Write a letter to your American penfriend to tell him/her about World Day – a multiracial day held in your school last week. Each class organized a different activity which included :

- cooking food from different countries
- playing music from around the world
- presenting clothes from different countries

D. SKILLS AND TECHNIQUES *22 pts*

1 *Pass on the information.* *10 pts*

Unten stehend findest du einen Auszug aus einer Fernsehreportage, in der Mat Kelley über die Projekte berichtet, die MAVIN organisiert. Was wird über die unten genannten 5 Aspekte ausgesagt?

"MAVIN magazine appears 4 times a year. It's based in Seattle and we have about 48,000 readers – the number's growing all the time. We also run the MAVIN FOUNDATION which organizes and sponsors projects. One of these projects was the Generation MIX tour. Five young multiracial people toured the USA in a bus and visited 17 university campuses. They wanted to talk to people about multiracial issues and they were filmed discussing with university students.

Another big project is the Matchmaker Bone Marrow Project. When people are ill and need a transplant operation, doctors need to find donors (people who give an organ of their body to help cure someone who is ill.) Because multiracial people are born with a complicated set of genes, it is very difficult to find multiracial donors who have exactly the same genes. So the Bone Marrow Project was set up to help find them.

The Foundation has also published a book called The Multiracal Advice Book. This gives advice and information to families about their children's education, health and problems. It's certainly had a lot of success.

In recent years, society has changed its attitude to multiracial people. And we like to believe that MAVIN has changed multiracial people's attitudes towards themselves. They realize more and more that they are not just half this or half that. Everyone – whatever their colour and their mix of races – is a complete individual with a wealth of diverse cultures. (244 words)

1. der Unterschied zwischen MAVIN und der MAVIN Foundation
2. die Ziele, die die Generation MIX tour verfolgt
3. die Aktivitäten des Bone-Marrow-Projekts
4. die Schwierigkeiten, Organspender zu finden
5. der Sinn des 'multiracial advice book'

Matchmaker Bone Marrow Projekt: *ein Projekt, das Menschen mit identischer Zusammensetzung des Knochenmarks und anderer Spenderorgane ausfindig macht.*

2 *Translate the following paragraph (lines 1 through 11, page 46) into German.* **12** *pts*

When Matt Kelley was growing up in the United States, he often thought to himself, "Who am I?". Of course, there is nothing unusual about this; most teenagers ask themselves the same question from time to time. But Matt's problem was special. When he saw his schoolmates, he didn't see anyone who looked like him. There were white kids and black kids, Asian kids and Hispanic kids*, but none like him. And when Matt went home and switched on the TV or opened a magazine, he still didn't see anyone who was quite like him.

____

____

____

____

____

____

____

____

***Hispanic kids:** *Braucht nicht übersetzt zu werden.*

E. SPELLING CHECK *6 pts*

1 ***Homophones***
Choose the correct words in each sentence. **6** *pts*

1. I'm sure that's the man ***who's/whose*** dog bit my sister last ***weak/week.***
2. I hope the ***weather/whether*** will be good this weekend because ***were/we're*** going away.
3. The players walked ***passed/past*** and ***there/their*** fans cheered loudly.
4. You should ***write/right*** your name ***here/hear*** at the top.
5. I'm still hungry because I only had a small ***piece/peace*** of meet/meat.
6. Men aren't ***aloud/allowed*** to have long ***hair/hare*** in the army.

7 Australian Connection

After passing his exams 18-year-old Alex decided to travel to Australia to visit his father Tom who he hadn't seen since his parents were divorced fifteen years ago.

To get to know each other father and son went on a trip to Queensland. On their way they had to stop at a river that crossed the road. A sign said:

DANGER – CROCODILES!

Fortunately, Tom was not eaten by a crocodile. Even more fortunately, at its deepest, the water only came up to Tom's knees, and the four-wheel drive crossed the river with no problems. Two hours later, they arrived at a hostel, deep within the rain forest at the foot of Mount Sorrow.

The next couple of days went far too quickly for Alex. He and Tom went walking through the steaming rain forest; they followed the boardwalk through the mangrove swamp; they rode horses along the sandy beach; they visited a crocodile reserve. Alex found himself surrounded by birds and insects, trees and flowers that he had only ever seen before on television.

"It's fantastic!" Alex said, again and again, as he saw more and more wonderful sights. "Really fantastic!"

"I'm glad you like it," said Tom. "I love it here. The trouble is, it's all changing. People from the cities are buying up the land and building holiday homes. Slowly but surely, the forest is being destroyed."

Alex looked at Tom. The trip had been wonderful so far. And yet it was not how Alex had imagined it would be. He felt somehow that he had lost a father, but found a friend.

After a final walk – to the top of Mount Sorrow – Tom and Alex packed up the four-wheel drive and left. By midday, they were back at the river which had been so full and fast before. Now, it was just a shallow stream and Tom drove across easily.

Alex turned and looked back through the rear-window at the rain forest. Beautiful and remote, it had remained untouched for thousands of years. Now, all that had changed, and if strict laws were not soon made, the rain forest and everything in it would disappear for ever.

"It's so sad," he said.

Tom nodded. "People can be very, very stupid," he agreed angrily.

As they left the rain forest behind and the roads improved, Tom began to cheer up. He told Alex all about Gypsy Women, the boat he shared with his brother, which was moored in Cairns.

"I thought we'd take her out onto the reef," he said.

"The Great Barrier Reef," Alex said excitedly.

"That's the one," Tom smiled.

Alex grinned. He knew all about the Great Barrier Reef, of course. He'd learnt about it in geography lessons and had always wanted to see the multi-coloured coral for himself. Now he was going to do just that.

"Is it as wonderful as it looks on film?" he asked.

"Better," Tom answered. "A million times better."

(493 words)

46 moored: *vor Anker lag*

This text is an extract from "The Australian Connection" by Paul Stewart, Cornelsen 1994, p. 36-37.

A. TEXT BASED TASKS *25 pts*

1

After you have read the text, read the following extract from the diary that Alex kept during his Australian trip. 13 of the facts are wrong. Underline the incorrect words and write down the correct facts at the end of the line. The first one is done for you. **13** *pts*

"The water came above Tom's knees so we could walk across the river easily — *up to* (1) ___ 2 ___

It took us all afternoon to reach the hostel at the top of Mount Sorrow. ___ 3 ___ ___ 4 ___

The next seven days were fantastic. We rode horses through the rain forest; ___ 5 ___ ___ 6 ___

we walked along the beach, and we visited a crocodile reserve. Everywhere I went ___ 7 ___

I saw amazing insects, birds, flowers and trees I had only read about before. ___ 8 ___

On the final day we walked down Mount Sorrow and arrived back at the river ___ 9 ___

by the evening. It was strange how the river, so shallow on our first ___ 10 ___ ___ 11 ___

day, was now very full and we only just managed to drive across. Tom has promised ___ 12 ___ ___ 13 ___

to take me to the Great Barrier Reef. I'm really looking forward to seeing it!

2

A reporter is asking Tom questions about the rain forest. Write down Tom's answers. The answers are not necessarily in the text. **4** *pts*

1. Why do a lot of city people buy up land in the rain forest?

___

2. How can they be stopped from doing this?

___

3. What will happen if they continue?

___

4. What's your opinion on people who do this?

___

3

Ask questions. **8** *pts*

Alex is phoning his mother back in the UK. She's eager to know how the trip is going. Write down two questions she asks Alex about his trip and two questions about his relationship with his father, Tom. Use at least three different question forms.

___

___

___

___

B. USE OF LANGUAGE *20 pts*

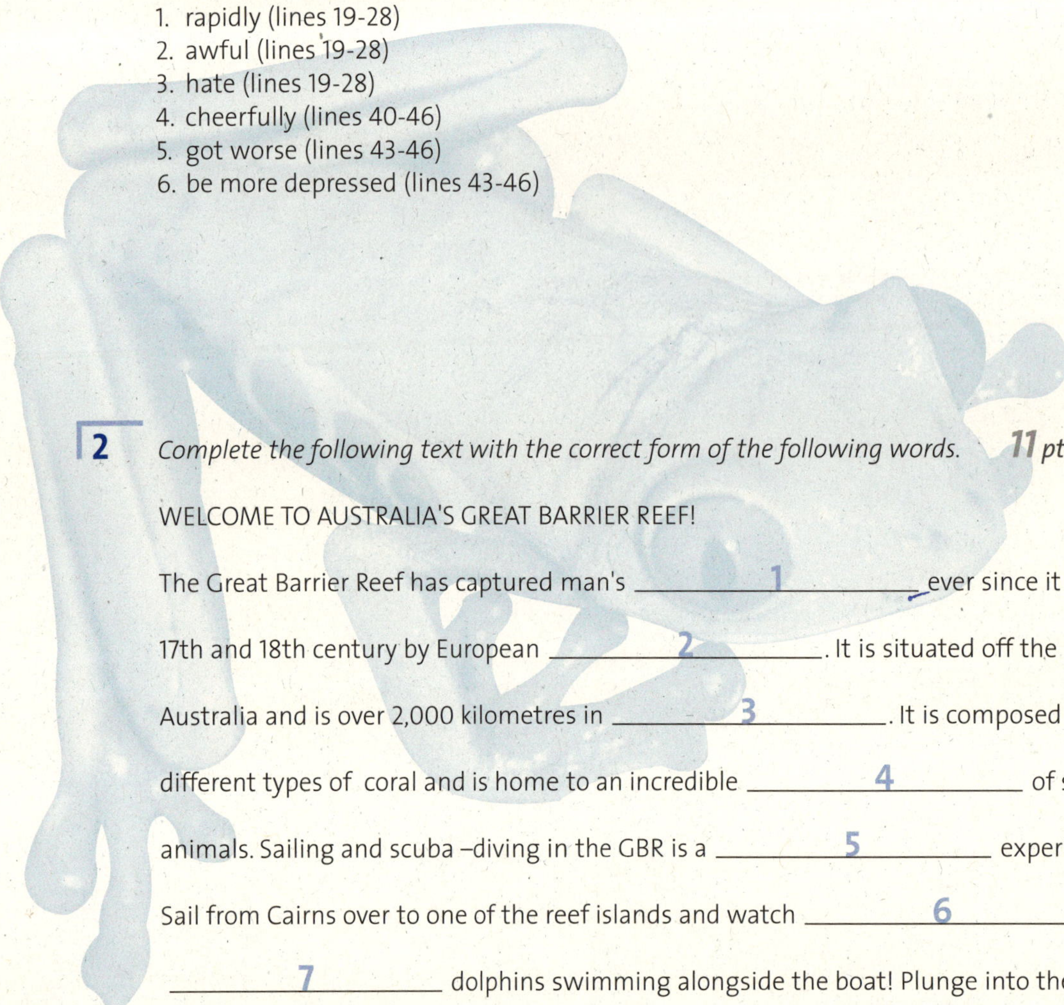

1 *Find the opposite of these words and phrases in the text.* *6 pts*

1. rapidly (lines 19-28)
2. awful (lines 19-28)
3. hate (lines 19-28)
4. cheerfully (lines 40-46)
5. got worse (lines 43-46)
6. be more depressed (lines 43-46)

2 *Complete the following text with the correct form of the following words.* *11 pts*

WELCOME TO AUSTRALIA'S GREAT BARRIER REEF!

The Great Barrier Reef has captured man's ______ 1 ______ ever since it was discovered in the 17th and 18th century by European ______ 2 ______. It is situated off the north east coast of Australia and is over 2,000 kilometres in ______ 3 ______. It is composed of hundreds of different types of coral and is home to an incredible ______ 4 ______ of sea plants and animals. Sailing and scuba –diving in the GBR is a ______ 5 ______ experience! Sail from Cairns over to one of the reef islands and watch ______ 6 ______ whales and ______ 7 ______ dolphins swimming alongside the boat! Plunge into the clear turquoise water and swim along with shoals of ______ 8 ______ coloured fish! Walk along the long white ______ 9 ______ beaches looking for shells and coral. The Great Barrier Reef has taken thousands of years to evolve but is a very fragile environment. This is why it is protected by the Australian Government who ______ 10 ______ ensure that it is used in the least harmful but the most enjoyable way by the large numbers of ______ 11 ______ who visit the area every year.

1.	imagine	4.	vary	7.	play	10.	sure
2.	explore	5.	memory	8.	bright	11.	tour
3.	long	6.	friend	9.	sand		

3 ***Prepositions*** *3 pts*

Complete the sentences with the prepositions listed below.

1. He dived into the cold water and swam ____?____ the river.
2. I saw her come ____?____ the cinema while I was waiting in the queue.
3. The local people are fed up with heavy lorries driving ____?____ their village!
4. "The station? You go ____?____ this road and it's on the left."
5. I cycled ____?____ the bridge as fast as I could.
6. As the boat sailed into shore, he jumped out ____?____ the sand.

through	across	onto	over	along	out of

C. CREATIVE WRITING *27 pts*

1 *What advice would you give to someone going on the same trip to the rain forest as Alex?* *9 pts*
Suggest useful objects to take and the right clothes to wear. Write about 60 words

2 *Choose task A **or** B. Write about 120 words.* **19** *pts*

*A. Tom is back from his trip to the rain forest. In Brisbane, he meets a man called Bob who has recently bought some land in the rain forest and is going to build a holiday house there. Tom and Bob start arguing. Think of good arguments for both sides and write a dialogue. **To help you, read the information about rain forests in section D1** (Pass on the information).*

Start like this:

Tom: Why have you chosen to buy land in the rain forest?
Bob: Because it's cheap, and nice and quiet! Not many people there.
Tom: What are you going to do on this land?
Bob: ...

B. Imagine you're Alex. Write a letter to your Dad, thanking him for the holiday you spent with him. Talk about the things you did, the moments you liked best and your feelings for him.

D. SKILLS AND TECHNIQUES **22** *pts*

1 ***Pass on the information.*** **12** *pts*

Auf einer Kundgebung in England hast du ein Flugblatt mit dem Titel RAIN FORESTS IN DANGER erhalten. Da die Information interessant ist, möchtest du deinem Freund zu Hause eine E-Msail zu folgenden Aspekten schicken
- die Bedeutung der Regenwälder
- Gründe für die Zerstörung der Regenwälder
- Wem gehören die Regenwälder und wer sollte von ihnen profitieren?
- Was verlangen die Autoren des Flugblatts?

The Amazon rain forest is being destroyed! Stop this destruction!
We need rain forests!Look at these important facts:

- The Amazon rain forest produces 20% of the oxygen that we breathe on this earth!
- The plants in the forest change carbon dioxide into clean air. This helps fight pollution and prevents the earth warming up – the greenhouse effect.
- TheAmazon rain forest contains an enormous diversity of plants and animals - many of which are found nowhere else on earth!
- the Amazon rain forest and surrounding regions contain 30% of the world's fresh water!
- the Amazon rain forest has plants that are used in medicine. 60% of the drugs which fight cancer and other deadly diseases come from plants that can only be found in the rain forest.
- The Amazon rain forest will become dry desert if the trees are cut down!

The soil on the ground of a rain forest does not contain many nutrients.They remain in the trees and plants. So when these are cut down, crops do not grow well and the soil erodes and dries out!

Who is destroying the rain forest?

- o Big ranchers. They clear huge areas of the forests to feed cattle and sell the meat to hamburger companies.
- o Rich logging companies. They cut down thousands of trees. They sell the wood pulp to be made into paper to feed the world with newspapers, magazines and paper products. They sell the wood to make cheap furniture.
- o Big multionational companies. They buy huge areas of land to pump oil.

A lot of these activities are illegal. Most of the rain forest is public land. The big companies do not have the right to exploit it.

There are many poor people living in or near the rain forest.They should be allowed to use a small part of the land to grow food for their families. But the big companies chase them away.

WE DEMAND STRICT LAWS TO PROTECT THE RAIN FOREST AND THE LOCAL INHABITANTS!
THE WORLD NEEDS RAIN FORESTS FOR ITS SURVIVAL!
STOP THE DAMAGE NOW BEFORE IT IS TOO LATE! (345 words)

2 *Translate the following paragraph (lines 43 through 56, page 52) into German.* ***10** pts*

As they left the rain forest behind and the roads improved, Tom began to cheer up. He told Alex all about 'Gypsy Woman', the boat he shared with his brother, which was moored in Cairns.
"I thought we'd take her out onto the reef," he said.
"The Great Barrier Reef?" Alex said excitedly.
"That's the one," Tom smiled.
Alex grinned. He knew all about the Great Barrier Reef, of course. He'd learnt about it in geography lessons and had always wanted to see the multi-coloured coral for himself. Now he was going to do just that.
"Is it as wonderful as it looks on film?" he asked.
"Better," Tom answered. "A million times better." (113 words)

E. SPELLING CHECK *6 pts*

1 ***s, 's or s' ?*** ***6** pts*
Put the apostrophies where you think it is necessary and rewrite the words in their correct forms.

1. Heres a red scarf. It must be yours, Mike. ______
2. Janes bikes gone! Whos stolen it? ______
3. When its dinnertime in our house, the cat miaows for its dinner, too. ______
4. All the pupils parents came to the school meeting except hers. ______
5. She put mens shirts, womens shoes and childrens toys in the Red Cross bags. ______
6. Theres a photo of James favourite football player in todays newspaper. ______

8 The Millau Bridge

When we think of a project to build a new bridge, we generally think of it as a feat of engineering skill rather than the work of an architect. However, the Millau Bridge in southern France was actually the idea of an architect, and its climbing, butterfly-like design and minimalist construction techniques may well change forever the way we think about engineering.

The architect was Sir Norman Foster, who is probably best known for his reconstruction of Berlin's Reichstag, and he had the help of one of France's oldest and most respected builders, the Eiffage construction group, who also built the Eiffel Tower. It took Foster and Eiffage over 10 years to plan and build the Millau Bridge, and the result, opened in December of 2004, is one of the longest bridges of its type, and the single tallest road bridge in the world.

The plan was to link Paris to the Mediterranean by high-speed motorway, but the River Tarn in the Massif Central was a serious problem: the Tarn cuts a deep valley between two high plateaus, and traffic had to go down one side of the valley and up the other in order to get across. This caused colossal traffic jams, especially in the summer months, and the effect on the local villages and the environment was less than ideal.

When Foster and Eiffage studied the issue, they realized that simply putting a new bridge over the Tarn wouldn't solve even half the problem: the traffic would still have to cross through the valley, and the construction itself would only worsen the pollution and general chaos in the area. So their solution was this: Why not build a bridge linking the two high plateaus, nearly 300 metres above the River Tarn? Yes, the bridge would need to be longer, but the total damage to the valley would be much less.

Despite its enormous size, the Millau Bridge has an elegant, almost transparent quality which harmonizes with the surrounding landscape. Perhaps more importantly, it was built with a minimum of materials and without doing damage to the environment. And the drive between Paris and the Mediterranean has been shortened by two hours. Norman Foster once said, "Great architecture should wear its message lightly." Perhaps the same could be said of great engineering.

(383 words)

A. TEXT BASED TASKS *22 pts*

1 *You are talking to Sir Norman Foster.* ***12** pts*
Ask him questions about the Millau Bridge. Write down 6 questions using at least three different question forms.

1
2
3
4
5
6

2 *Find the information in the text.* ***5** pts*

1. Before the Millau Bridge was built, how did traffic cross the River Tarn?

___

2. What happened when the traffic crossed the old bridge over the Tarn?

___

3. Why didn't Sir Norman simply replace the old bridge over the Tarn with a new bridge?

___

4. To solve the problems, what sort of bridge did he decide to build?

___

5. In which way has the new bridge given great advantage to people driving from the north to the south of France?

___

3 *Complete the sentences.* ***5** pts*

1. Bridges are usually designed by ___?___ rather than by ___?___.
2. The Millau Bridge is part of a plan to ___?___.
3. The Bridge holds two world records: ___?___.
4. The Millau Bridge has been designed to harmonize with ___?___.
5. The construction of the bridge hardly didn't do any harm ___?___.

B. USE OF LANGUAGE *22 pts*

1 *Choose three of the following words and phrases and explain their meaning.* *8 pts*

1. minimalist (line 6)
2. to link (line 18)
3. colossal (line 23)
4. chaos (line 32)

2 *Read the following text and look carefully at each line.* *8 pts*
Some of the lines are correct, but some aren't. If the line is correct, put a tick. If not, write down the incorrect word .

How high is high?

1. The highest building in the world used to be the Empire State Building	?
2. at 381 meters. Built in 1931 in New York, it was the most tallest for	?
3. 41 years until in 1973 when the World Trade Center (417 meters) was	?
4. finished. A year later, in 1974, the Sears Tower in Chicago was being built	?
5. which went up to a height of 442 meters. It remained the world's highest	?
6. skyscraper for 24 years. Up to that date, skyscrapers were specifically	?
7. American but then the rest of the world started to wanting them, too.	?
8. The next one skyscrapers to be built were the Petronas Towers in Malaysia	?
9. in 1998. Two oriental-style twin towers do reach up to 452 meters!	?
10. After that, one skyscraper followed to another in quick succession: the	?
11. Jin Mao Tower in Shanghai in 1999, followed by the Finance Center in	?
12. Hong Kong in 2003 and the Taipei 101 in Taiwan in 2004 – today's	?
13. world record-breaker at 508 metres – that's over half of a kilometre!	?
14. And there two more are planned for 2008 and 2009: Freedom Tower	?
15. in New York and the giant of them all, Burj Dubai in the Middle East, an	?
16. incredible 600 meters high!	?

3 ***Making verbs from adjectives.*** *6 pts*

Look at these two verbs from the text formed from adjectives:

to worsen (worse) to shorten (short)

Complete the sentences with the verb formed from indicated adjectives.

1. In the nineteenth century, the canal was ___WIDE___ to allow large boats to travel along it.
2. The scary music in the film last night ___HIGH___ the atmosphere of suspense.
3. Runways in some airports will have to be ___LONG___ so that the new Airbus can land.
4. That's a very funny photo of you! You should get it ___LARGE___ into a poster!
5. The cement ___HARD___ quickly so you'll have to work fast!
6. The goal-posts aren't solid enough – you'll need to ___STRONG___ them.

C. CREATIVE WRITING *29 pts*

1 ***What advice would you give?*** *9 pts*

Choose ***two*** *of the following situations and give advice to your friend. Write about 60 words.*

1. Your friend has to cycle home at night on a busy road.
2. Your friend has had a mobile telephone for his/her birthday.
3. Your friend wants to find out where to do a canoeing course during the holiday.

2 *Choose 2A* ***or*** *2B. Write about 120 words.* *20 pts*

A. Write an article about a building in your town or village. Describe it and say why you like it or why you don't like it.

B. Write a story which starts like this:
"Yesterday morning my alarm didn't go off."
... and finishes like this:
"What a stroke of luck that I got up late that day!"

D. SKILLS AND TECHNIQUES 22 pts

1 Pass on the information. 10 pts

Unten stehend findest du einen Text zum Thema "Brücken auf den Euro-Geldscheinen". Beantworte die unten stehenden Fragen auf Deutsch.

Bridges on the Euro banknotes

Have you ever looked closely at a euro banknote?
The front and the back?

Are there famous faces from European history or famous monuments in Europe? The answer is 'no'.
On the front of each euro banknote is a picture of a window or a gateway, and on the back of each note is a ... bridge!
There are seven denominations of banknotes (5, 10, 20, 50, 100, 200 and 500 euros) and each one has a different bridge. But these aren't real bridges which exist somewhere in Europe. They're invented bridges – to symbolize the link between people and countries. So how did a bridge get onto the euro banknotes and who designed it?

In February 1996, six years before the launch of the euro, a competition was held to find the best design for the euro banknote. Forty-four designs were proposed and they were judged by a jury of fourteen experts. The winning design was chosen in December 1996. It was by an artist called Robert Kalina, a banknote designer at the Austrian National Bank. He proposed seven bridges representing seven periods of European history – from Roman times up to the present day. A Roman viaduct is represented on the smallest banknote of 5 euros and you can follow the historical evolution of architecture through consecutive banknotes right up to a very modern bridge on the 500 euro note. On the front of the note there is designed a window or a gateway in the same style symbolizing communication between the member countries. Why didn't Robert Kalina draw bridges that already existed? Simply because certain banknotes would be associated with specific countries and that, of course, would go against the spirit of the European Union! (285 words)

1. Welche Darstellungen findet man auf der Vorder- und Rückseite der Euro-Noten?
2. Die Darstellungen auf der Rückseite der Banknoten gibt es nicht in Wirklichkeit. Kannst du erklären, weshalb das so ist?
3. Was steht im Text über das Auswahlverfahren bei der Gestaltung der Banknoten?
4. Wer hat diese Banknoten entworfen?
5. Wie wurden die Entwürfe ausgewählt?

2 *Translate the following paragraph (lines 9 through 20, page 58) into German.* 12 pts

The architect was Sir Norman Foster, who is probably best known for his reconstruction of Berlin's Reichstag, and he had the help of one of France's oldest and most respected builders, the Eiffage [1] construction group, who also built the Eiffel Tower. It took Foster and Eiffage over 10 years to plan and build the Millau Bridge, and the result, opened in December of 2004, is one of the longest bridges of its type, and the single tallest road bridge in the world. The plan was to link Paris to the Mediterranean by high-speed motorway, but the River Tarn in the Massif Central [2] was a serious problem.

1 ***Eiffage*** *braucht nicht übersetzt zu werden*
2 ***Massif Central*** *Zentralmassiv*

E. SPELLING CHECK 6 pts

1 ***Suffixes*** 3 *pts*

Read the following letter and correct the six mistakes in the underlined words..

Dear Mr and Mrs Johnson,

I am writeing to thank you very much for haveing me to stay. It was extremely kind of you and I appreciated your driving me around to show me all the interesting sights. I got back to Cologne safely.

At the moment I am looking for a new apartment and I visited two yesterday. One was on the nineth floor with a lovly view but it was very small. I can't imagine living in such a small space. The other was bigger but needed a lot of improvments made. Hopefully, I will find the perfect one before the end of the week!

Again, thankyou for everything.
Hoping you'll be comeing to visit us soon.

Yours sincerely
Anna

1. ______________________ 4. ______________________

2. ______________________ 5. ______________________

3. ______________________ 6. ______________________

2 ***Suffixes*** 3 *pts*

Add the correct suffix – 'ary', 'ery' or 'ory' - to the indicated words.

1. The police are investigating an armed ______ ROBB ______ that took place at the bank yesterday.
2. Indians attacked the early American cowboys to protect their ______ TERRIT ______.
3. The ______ DISCOV ______ of penicillin was a great leap forward in medicine.
4. You'll find 'Lord of the Rings' and other works by Tolkien in the local ______ LIBR ______.
5. In a lot of countries in the world young people still have to do ______ MILIT ______ service.
6. There is a new ______ FACT ______ being built on the outskirts of the town.

Abschlussprüfung Englisch

Erarbeitet von:
Günter Hanisch
(Lerntipps und Beratung)
Dave Humphreys
(Texte: Sailing Teens, Earth Day, Surfing with Sharks, One Who Understands, Millau Bridge)
Rachel Thomas
(sämtliche Übungen)

Beratung:
Gabriele Künstler
Sibille Renz-Noll
Angelika Spitzmüller

Redaktion und technische Umsetzung:
Klaus Blocher
Eri Koizumi

Layoutgestaltung:
werkstatt für gebrauchsgrafik, Berlin

Umschlaggestaltung:
hawemannundmosch, bureau für gestaltung, Berlin

Bild- und Textquellen:
S. 16
Text: Reproduced by permission of Oxford University Press from New Headway Intermediate the new edition Students Book by John and Liz Soars © Oxford University Press 2003
S. 16, 46, 58
Photo unten: Corbis, Deutschland
S. 22
Text und Photos: Theodora Children's Trust, London, www.theodora.org.uk

www.cornelsen.de

1. Auflage, 2. Druck 2005

Druck: CS-Druck CornelsenStürtz, Berlin

ISBN-13: 978-3-06-031092-0
ISBN-10: 3-06-031092-0

Inhalt gedruckt auf Recyclingpapier, hergestellt aus 100 % Altpapier.

B. story
Yesterday morning my alarm didn't go off and I woke up late! I ran down the stairs, putting on my clothes and picking up my bag and raced to the bus stop. I was too late – the bus was disappearing down the road! So I started walking. Just then, a car stopped and the driver asked me directions to Langley Sports Club. His face looked familiar. I explained how to get there and he handed me an envelope and said "Thanks very much. This is for you and a friend". Then he drove off. I opened the envelope. There were two tickets for Saturday's football match against Arsenal! What a stroke of luck I got up late and missed the bus! (121 words)

D. Skills and Techniques *page 62*

1
1. Auf der Vorderseite der Euro-Noten findet sich die Darstellung eines Fensters oder eines Portals; auf der Rückseite sind Brücken abgebildet.
2. Die sieben dargestellten Brücken entsprechen verschiedenen Epochen der europäischen Geschichte. Es handelt sich aber nicht um reale Brücken, da man den Hinweis auf einzelne Mitgliedsländer vermeiden wollte. Schließlich ging es darum, Brücken als völker- und länderverbindende Symbole abzubilden.
3. Im Februar 1996, also deutlich vor Einführung des Euro, fand ein Wettbewerb für die Gestaltung der Banknoten statt. Dabei wurden insgesamt 44 Entwürfe eingereicht.
4. Der Entwurf unserer jetzigen Banknoten stammt von dem Österreicher Robert Kalina, der für die österreichische Nationalbank als Designer tätig ist.
5. Eine 14-köpfige Jury wählte den besten unter den 44 Entwürfen aus. Dies geschah 10 Monate nach Einreichung der Vorschläge.

2 Der Architekt ist Sir Normann Foster, der wahrscheinlich vor allem für seine Neugestaltung des Berliner Reichstags bekannt ist, und er wurde unterstützt von einem der ältesten und berühmtesten Bauunternehmen Frankreichs, nämlich der Eiffage-Gruppe, die auch den Eiffelturm gebaut hat. Foster und Eiffage brauchten über 10 Jahre, um die Brücke zu planen und umzusetzen. Das Resultat, das im Dezember 2004 eröffnet wurde, ist eine der längsten Brücken dieser Art und die höchste Straßenbrücke weltweit.
Geplant war, Paris und das Mittelmeer durch eine Schnellstraße zu verbinden, aber der Fluss Tarn im Zentralmassiv stellte ein ernsthaftes Problem dar.

E. Spelling Check *page 63*

1
1. writing
2. having
3. ninth
4. lovely
5. improvements
6. coming

2
1. robbery
2. territory
3. discovery
4. library
5. military
6. factory